Fresh & Ta

Potato
recipes

R&R PUBLICATIONS MARKETING PTY LTD

Published by:
R&R Publications Marketing Pty Ltd
ABN 78 348 105 138
PO Box 254, Carlton North, Victoria 3054 Australia
Phone (61 3) 9381 2199 Fax (61 3) 9381 2689
E-mail: info@randrpublications.com.au
Website: www.randrpublications.com.au
Australia wide toll-free: 1800 063 296

Fresh & Tasty Potato recipes

Publisher: Richard Carroll
Creative Director: Aisling Gallagher
Cover Designer: Lucy Adams
Typesetter: Elain Wei Voon Loh
Production Manager: Anthony Carroll
Food Photography: Steve Baxter, Phillip Wilkins, David Munns, Thomas Odulate,
Christine Hanscomb and Frank Wieder
Home Economists: Sara Buenfeld, Emma Patmore, Nancy McDougall, Louise Pickford,
Jane Stevenson, Oded Schwartz, Alison Austin and Jane Lawrie
Food Stylists: Helen Payne, Sue Russell, Sam Scott, Antonia Gaunt and Oded Schwartz
Recipe Development: Terry Farris, Jacqueline Bellefontaine, Becky Johnson, Valerie Barrett, Emma
Patmore, Geri Richards, Pam Mallender and Jan Fullwood
Proofreader: Paul Hassing

Disclaimer: The nutritional information listed with each recipe does not include the nutrient content
of garnishes or any accompaniments not listed in specific quantities in the ingredient list. The
nutritional information for each recipe is an estimate only, and may vary depending on the brand of
ingredients used, and due to biological variations in the composition of natural foods such as meat,
fish, fruit and vegetables. The nutritional information was calculated by using the computer
Foodworks dietary analysis software (version 3.01, Xyris Software Pty Ltd Queensland Australia),
and is based on the Australian food composition tables and food manufacturers' data. Where not
specified, ingredients are always analysed as average or medium, not small or large. The analysis
shown is for 100g of the recipe specified.

Includes Index
ISBN 978-1-74022-296-9

First Printed September 2002
Reprinted March 2004, July 2005 and January 2006
This Edition Printed February 2007
Computer Typeset in Futura

Printed in Singapore

Cover: Potato Feta Fritters, page 23

47

Contents

61

74

Introduction

The potato is one of the world's most popular vegetables, cultivated in almost every country. The many varieties native to different regions have different properties. As a result, the potato suits most culinary styles and is perhaps the most versatile staple food.

Russia, Poland and Germany are the highest potato consumers, followed by Holland, Cyprus and Ireland. On average we eat 60 kg per head per annum, which is good news when you consider the nutritional properties of this most loved tuber. The average 225g potato, contains 154 calories, has fibre, protein and starch for energy, only a quarter gram of fat and is a good source of Vitamin C.

Most of the vitamins are found just beneath the skin, which is why it's often suggested that potatoes are cooked in their skins and then peeled. If cooked without fat, the potato plays a great role in the slimming diet – a fact disputed in the past.

The potato has not always been held in such high regard. It originated in Peru, South America and is thought to date back as far as 3000 BC. First known as the 'papa' and eaten by the Incas, the potato was unknown to the rest of the world until the 16th century, when Spanish conquistador Francisco Pizarro captured Peru – famed for its mineral riches. The mineral trade brought many people to Peru, who in turn carried the potato to the rest of the world. It was known by many names, reflecting the different cooking methods used by the Indians. The potato was eaten fresh in season and dried for use in winter. Nowadays the storage life of potatoes and the different methods of preservation have increased its popularity.

The potato was first cultivated in Seville, Spain and then spread throughout Europe. Its name gradually changed form 'battata'. It became famous for its nutritional and healing properties – the Italians believed it could heal a wound if the cooked flesh was rubbed into the infected area. One person who fervently believed this was Pope Pious IV, who was sent potatoes when he was ill, then grew his own crop in Italy.

It then spread to Belgium, Germany, Switzerland and France, but did not reach the British Isles until Frances Drake stopped in the New World and shared his cargo (mainly potatoes) with the starving English colonists.

Later repatriated by Sir Walter Raleigh, the colonists brought the potato to Britain, where Raleigh grew the crop on his land. He was also responsible for taking the potato to Ireland, where the soil was perfect for growing it. The starving Irish soon adopted the potato as their own and it became a mainstay of their diet.

The first potatoes in Australia were grown in New South Wales in the early days of settlement. Whilst production was slow to get going, once established, it made great progress and is now a major primary industry.

Today there are many varieties of potato, each suitable for different cooking methods, be it roasting, boiling, steaming, baking, or frying. The potato is particularly versatile it readily absorbs other flavours and has a consistency that lends itself to many uses.

The wide array of recipes in this book will open up a world of delightful dishes, from hearty soups and salads to light snacks and accompaniments to marvellous main meals and beautiful bakes – There is something for everyone – whether you're dieting, a vegetarian or just a potato lover.

Types of Potato

There are around 3,000 known varieties of potato, but only 100 of these are regularly grown. Of these, only about 4 or 5 are found with ease on green grocer and supermarket shelves. However, if you look further afield into specialty shops you will be amazed at the different styles and tastes available.The following is a brief description of the most popular varieties and their uses, as a guide for the recipes in this book.

Bintje

Large oval tubers have pale yellow flesh which cooks without discolouration. Shallow eyes make them easy to prepare with minimum wastage.

Bison

Round, bright red tubers with good household cooking qualities.

Blue

Include such varieties as Blue Carib and All Blue. They have greyish blue skin and inky blue flesh. Delicate in flavour, they should simply be boiled and buttered.

Coliban

Smooth, white skinned tubers, producing high yield with little waste. The flesh has a waxy, slightly mealy texture and they store well. French fries are usually crisp and light coloured.

Delaware or White Rose

A long, firm, white waxy potato with a thin ivory-coloured skin. It's best for boiling but may be baked or roasted. It is not suitable for French fries or crisps.

Desirée

Hardy variety which produces good yields of pinkish-red-skinned tubers with pale yellow flesh. They store well and can be used for most culinary purposes.

Kennebec

Medium to large tubers are round and oval with white skin and flesh. Grown mainly for frozen French fries and crisps.

Pontiac

This type has a thin red skin and crisp white flesh. It is a waxy potato, excellent for boiling in the skin and serving whole. Because it cubes neatly after boiling and absorbs dressing readily, it's also good for potato salad. Red-skinned potatoes may also be rubbed with olive oil and baked whole as they maintain their firm, waxy texture. They tend to be dark, limp and oily when fried.

Russet Burbank or Idaho

This standard baking potato is generally 10–15cm long and 5cm in diameter, with a rough brown skin. The ivory flesh is dry and fluffy when baked. It is a good potato for mashing and for deep-frying, as it's high water content means it doesn't readily absorb frying oil.

Sebago

Most commonly grown fresh market and processing variety in total. Good, general purpose potato for domestic use and for crisp manufacture.

Tarago

Produces blocky tubers, ideal for the crisps and fries.

Tasman

Pale red skinned variety that yields well and is more tolerant of tuber damage than other varieties.

Selection

The most important distinction in potato varieties is between the floury or mealy types (best for baking) and the waxy types (best for boiling). Floury types fall apart when boiled; waxy types don't develop the desired dry, fluffy texture when baked.

When selecting potatoes, look for firm specimens. New potatoes should be of a fairly uniform size to make cooking easier. Mature baking potatoes should be dry and well shaped, without sprouting.

Potatoes with a greenish cast or sprouted 'eyes' indicate exposure to light or storage at too high or too low a temperature. Both can be highly toxic and should not be eaten. If potatoes start to sprout during storage, remove the sprouts with a sharp knife, cutting deeply around the eyes before cooking the potatoes immediately.

Storage

Potatoes are best stored in a cool, dark, dry place, where they should keep for two to three weeks without sprouting. Don't refrigerate them.

Preparation

Peel if you wish, or scrub the skin well. Potatoes oxidise quickly, so drop peeled potatoes into water immediately to slow browning.

Soups
and Starters

Potato forms the basis of many delicious easy-to-prepare soups, as it's the perfect thickening ingredient and adds a subtle flavour.
With the addition of just a few ingredients, you have a whole selection of inexpensive soups at your fingertips. Add herbs, onion, garlic, meat, fish or vegetables, top with herbs or croûtons or simply serve with crusty bread for anything from a light starter to a filling meal.

Curried Sweet Potato Soup

Preparation 20 mins **Cooking** 50–75 mins **Calories** 146 **Fat** 2g

2 tsps canola oil
½ carrot, diced
½ onion, diced
1 stalk celery, diced
1 clove garlic, crushed
2 tsps curry powder
½ tsp cumin seeds
½ tsp yellow mustard seeds
2 tbsps chopped fresh coriander
4 cups low-salt vegetable stock
½ cup beer or stout
1 tbsp honey
455g orange sweet potato, chopped
½ tsp ground cinnamon
1 sugar banana, chopped (optional)
lime wedges, to serve

Lime Yogurt
½ cup low-fat natural yogurt
2 tsps finely grated lime zest
2 tsps lime juice

1 Heat the oil in a saucepan over a medium heat. Add the carrot, onion, celery and garlic. Cook, stirring, for 3 minutes. Stir in the curry powder and cumin and mustard seeds. Cook until the mustard seeds start to pop.

2 Add the coriander, stock, beer and honey. Bring to the boil. Add the sweet potato, cinnamon and banana (if using). Simmer, stirring occasionally, until the sweet potato is soft. Cool slightly.

3 Transfer the mixture to a food processor or blender. Purée in batches. Return the mixture to a clean saucepan. Reheat.

4 To make the lime yogurt, place the yogurt and lime zest and juice in a small bowl. Mix to combine.

5 To serve, ladle the soup into warm bowls. Top with a spoonful of Lime yogurt. Serve with lime wedges.

Serves 6

Note: The banana creates a unique flavour that you may or may not like. The soup is still divine without it.

German Potato Soup with Cauliflower and Caraway

Preparation 20 mins **Cooking** 1–1½ hrs **Calories** 210 **Fat** 2g

1 bunch spring onions, sliced

2 tbsps olive oil

1 medium cauliflower head, cut into florets (reserve small florets)

570g white potatoes, peeled and diced

1 tsp caraway seeds, plus extra for garnish

6 cups vegetable stock

2 tbsps mild yogurt

1 Cut 5cm lengths off the end of each spring onion. Using a sharp knife, slice these into thin strips, keeping one end intact to hold the strips together. Plunge the strips into a bowl of iced water and set aside until they curl, about 1 hour.

2 Heat the olive oil in a large saucepan and add the remaining spring onion, sliced diagonally, and sauté for a few seconds. Add the cauliflower florets, potatoes and caraway seeds and sauté for 10 minutes until golden.

3 Add the stock and bring the soup to the boil. Simmer for 45 minutes then process with a food processor or hand-held 'wand' until smooth.

4 Add the reserved small cauliflower florets and simmer for 10 minutes.

5 Serve the soup with a little dob of yogurt, a sprinkling of caraway seeds and the spring onion curls.

Serves 6

Glamorgan Sausages with Tomato Salad

Preparation 20 mins + 15 mins cooling + 1 hr chilling **Cooking** 3 mins **Calories** 540 **Fat** 35g

100g floury potato
100g white breadcrumbs
145g Lancashire or Caerphilly cheese, grated
1 small leek, finely chopped
¼ tsp dried sage
1 tbsp chopped fresh parsley
salt and black pepper
pinch of cayenne pepper
1 medium egg, plus 2 egg yolks
4 tbsps plain flour
oil for shallow frying

Salad

4 tbsps olive oil
2 tsps balsamic vinegar
pinch of brown sugar
145g cherry tomatoes
1 red onion, thinly sliced
5cm piece Lebanese cucumber, sliced
few fresh basil leaves

1 Cook the potato in boiling salted water for 15–20 minutes, until tender. Drain well, mash, then leave to cool for 15 minutes. Mix the cool mash with ½ the breadcrumbs and the cheese, leek, sage and parsley. Season with salt, pepper and cayenne. Bind together with the yolks. Using your hands, shape the mixture into 12 sausages. Cover and refrigerate for 1 hour.

2 Season the flour. Beat the whole egg. Dip the sausages into the seasoned flour, then into the beaten egg, then coat them in the remaining breadcrumbs. Heat 5mm of oil in a large frying pan and fry ½ the sausages, turning, for 10 minutes or until golden brown. Drain on absorbent paper and keep warm while you cook the rest.

Salad

1 Whisk together the oil, vinegar and sugar. Halve the tomatoes and toss in the dressing with the onion, cucumber and basil. Season and serve with the sausages.

Serves 4

Note: Glamorgan sausages are usually made with Caerphilly, but a good Lancashire produces equally delicious results.

Indian Curried Vegetable Soup

Preparation 25 mins **Cooking** 1–1½ hrs **Calories** 713 **Fat** 23g

2 tbsps butter or ghee
2 tsps turmeric
4 cloves garlic, ground
1 tbsp mild curry powder
1 tbsp garam masala
1 tbsp ground ginger
1 tsp chilli flakes
4 medium potatoes
2 sweet potatoes (kumera)
2 turnips
1 parsnip
4 medium carrots
1 medium butternut pumpkin
4 medium zucchini
400g peas, shelled
4 cups vegetable stock
400mL coconut milk
salt and pepper
1 cup coriander leaves, to garnish

1 Heat the butter or ghee and add the turmeric, garlic, curry powder, garam masala, ginger and chilli flakes and sauté until the spices are fragrant.

2 Meanwhile, peel and chop all the root vegetables and the pumpkin. Slice the zucchini and shell the peas.

3 Add the chopped vegetables (not the zucchini and peas) to the spice mixture, add the stock and bring the soup to the boil. Simmer for 45 minutes until the vegetables are very soft.

4 Add the coconut milk, zucchini and peas and continue to simmer for 15 minutes. Season with salt and pepper and serve, garnished with coriander and accompanied by toasted Indian bread and cucumber yogurt.

Serves 4

Portuguese Potato and Bean Soup

Preparation 40 mins **Cooking** 2–2½ hrs **Calories** 465 **Fat** 8g

4 cloves garlic, minced
2 medium onions, diced
2 medium carrots, diced
4 medium floury potatoes
1 green capsicum, finely diced
425g can Italian tomatoes, finely diced
½ medium green cabbage, sliced
425g can kidney beans, drained and rinsed
455g smoked Polish sausage, diced
6½ cups chicken stock
salt and pepper
2 tbsps chopped parsley, to garnish

1 Place all the ingredients in a large pot and bring to the boil. Reduce the heat to a simmer and partially cover with a lid.

2 Simmer for 2 hours, stirring occasionally. After 2 hours, add salt and pepper to taste and serve piping hot, garnished with parsley.

Serves 6–8

Note: You'll love the flavours in this satisfying soup. It's incredibly easy to prepare and makes a perfect Sunday night supper soup. Since this soup contains no oil, you can make it a regular, guilt-free indulgence.

Leek, Potato and Parsnip Chowder *(Not photographed)*

Preparation 20 mins **Cooking** 30 mins **Calories** 400 **Fat** 13g

30g butter
1 large leek, chopped
750g potatoes, peeled and diced
400g parsnips, peeled and diced
1¾ cups chicken stock
1 bay leaf
¼ tsp dried thyme
1 cup milk
8 rashers bacon, chopped
salt and pepper to taste

1 In a medium saucepan, melt the butter and then add leek, potatoes and parsnips and sauté over a medium high heat, stirring for 4 minutes. Pour in the stock and add bay leaf and thyme. Reduce the heat to low, cover and simmer for 15 minutes until vegetables are cooked.

2 Remove the pan from heat and with a potato masher crush the vegetables to thicken the chowder. Return to heat, stir in the milk and bring to the boil. Reduce heat and keep warm.

3 In a small frying pan, cook the bacon until crisp, drain and place bacon on kitchen paper.

4 Remove the bay leaf from the chowder and discard. Season the soup to taste with salt and pepper. Chop the bacon and sprinkle over the chowder to serve.

Serves 4

Lobster Topping

Preparation 5 mins **Cooking** none **Calories** 190 **Fat** 6g

115g cream cheese
115mL mayonnaise
55mL sour cream
2 tbsps fish stock
2 tsps lemon juice
½ clove garlic, crushed
1 tsp dried chives
255g lobster meat, diced
6–8 potatoes

1 Beat together the cream cheese, mayonnaise and sour cream. Add the lobster juice, lemon juice, garlic and chives. Beat well. Stir in the lobster meat. Serve over hot baked potatoes.

Serves 6–8

Pear Vichyssoise

Preparation 40 mins + chilling **Calories** 232 **Fat** 6g

200g dried pears

1 tbsp butter

1 leek, white part only, thinly sliced

1 small Spanish onion, thinly sliced

1 medium floury potato, peeled and sliced

5 cups water

2 tbsps chicken stock powder

285mL thickened cream

2cm piece fresh ginger root, for fresh ginger juice

¼ tsp nutmeg

sprigs of watercress, to garnish

1 Reserve 2 pear halves to garnish and roughly dice the rest. Melt the butter in a saucepan, add the leek and onion and stir to coat with the butter. Reduce the heat to very low, cover with a lid and allow to sweat until soft but not coloured (about 10 minutes).

2 Add the potato, diced pears, water and stock powder. Bring to the boil, then turn down the heat and simmer for 30 minutes. Cool the soup slightly and purée in a blender or food processor, or rub through a sieve. Place in a glass or stainless steel bowl.

3 Stir the cream into the soup and add 1–2 teaspoons of fresh ginger juice (see Tip) and the nutmeg. If the soup is too thick, add a little milk or liquid stock. Cover with plastic wrap and place in the refrigerator for several hours to chill. For best results, stand the bowl of soup in a basin of ice cubes in the refrigerator.

4 Finely dice the reserved pears. Garnish with a sprinkling of diced pear and a sprig of watercress.

Serves 6

Tip: To make fresh ginger juice, peel a 2cm piece of fresh ginger root, cut it into ½cm cubes and press the juice with a garlic crusher into a small bowl. Alternatively, grate a peeled piece of ginger with a fine grater onto a plate, then tilt the plate to let the juice run while pressing the fibre with the back of a spoon.

Potato Bacon Chowder

Preparation 30 mins **Cooking** 25–35 mins **Calories** 499 **Fat** 17g

225g bacon, chopped
30g butter
2 large onions, chopped
4 stalks celery, chopped
2 tsps dried thyme
2 tbsps plain flour
6 cups chicken stock
2 large potatoes, peeled and cubed
285mL sour cream
3 tbsps chopped fresh parsley
2 tbsps snipped fresh chives

1 Place the bacon in a large, heavy-based saucepan and cook over a medium heat for 5 minutes or until golden and crisp. Remove from the pan and drain on absorbent paper.

2 Melt the butter in the pan and cook the onions, celery and thyme over a low heat for 4–5 minutes or until the onion is soft.

3 Return the bacon to the pan, then stir in the flour and cook for 1 minute. Remove the pan from the heat and gradually blend in the stock. Bring to the boil, then reduce the heat. Add the potatoes and cook for 10 minutes or until they're tender.

4 Remove the pan from the heat and stir in the sour cream and parsley. Return to the heat and cook without boiling, stirring constantly, for 1–2 minutes. Ladle the soup the into bowls, sprinkle with chives and serve immediately.

Serves 6

Potato and Parsley Croquettes

Preparation 15 mins + 1 hr cooling **Cooking** 40 mins **Calories** 434 **Fat** 27g

85g long-grain rice
2 large potatoes, cut into chunks
2 red onions, finely chopped
1 clove garlic, crushed
4 tbsps chopped fresh parsley
salt and black pepper
6 tbsps sesame seeds
sunflower oil for frying

1   Cook the rice according to the packet instructions, until tender, then drain well. Spread it on a plate and leave for 1 hour or until completely cooled, fluffing it up with a fork occasionally.

2   Meanwhile, put the potatoes into a large saucepan of boiling salted water, then simmer for 15–20 minutes, until tender. Drain, then mash. Put the mashed potato into a large bowl with the cooled rice, onions, garlic, parsley and seasoning. Mix thoroughly.

3   Shape the mixture into 8 croquettes with your hands, then roll in the sesame seeds. Heat 1cm of oil in a large, heavy-based frying pan and fry the croquettes for 2–3 minutes, turning until crisp and browned all over.

Serves 4

Note: Crisp and golden outside and meltingly soft inside, these croquettes are very moreish. They're especially good served with a dollop of tangy tomato relish.

Potato Skins

baking potatoes

Bacon and Mushroom Topping

potato pulp

sautéed bacon and mushroom, chopped

parsley, chopped

Shrimp and Chive Topping

potato pulp

sour cream

chopped fresh chives

cooked prawns, chopped

salt and pepper

Chicken and Almond Topping

potato pulp

cooked chicken, chopped

toasted pine nuts, chopped

chopped shallots

sour cream

black pepper

1 Preheat the oven. Wash and dry each potato. Pierce with a fork and place in the preheated oven. Bake for 30 minutes or until the centre is firm but easily pierced with a fork.

2 Cool the potato, cut it in quarters lengthwise and cut out the centre, leaving the skin with 1–2cm of potato on it.

3 Brush the skins with butter, then sprinkle with salt and pepper. Bake for 10 minutes. Top with chosen topping and bake for another 5–10 minutes until warmed.

Makes 4 pieces per potato

Oven temperature 180°C

Potato Cakes with Smoked Salmon

Preparation 15 mins **Cooking** 40 mins **Calories** 303 **Fat** 18g

315g floury potatoes such as Idaho,
unpeeled

145mL full-fat milk

salt and black pepper

1 large egg

30g plain flour

4 spring onions, finely sliced

1 tbsp oil

115mL crème fraîche

2 tbsps chopped fresh dill, plus extra
to garnish

145g smoked salmon slices

lemon wedges, to garnish

1 Cook the potatoes in boiling salted water for 15–20 minutes, until tender, then drain. Cool for a few minutes, then peel. Mash with the milk, season, then beat in the egg, flour and spring onions to make a batter.

2 Heat a heavy-based non-stick frying pan, then add a little of the oil. Make 4 potato cakes, using 2 tablespoons of batter for each. Fry for 2–3 minutes each side until golden. Drain on absorbent paper and keep warm while you make 2 more batches of 4 potato cakes.

3 Mix together the crème fraîche and chopped dill. Serve the pancakes topped with the salmon and a spoonful of the herby crème fraîche. Grind over black pepper. Garnish with dill and lemon wedges.

Serves 4

Potato and Parsnip Puddings with Apple Sauce

Preparation 30 mins + 20 mins chilling **Cooking** 3 mins **Calories** 211 **Fat** 7g

Puddings

40g potatoes, peeled and coarsely grated

145g parsnips, peeled and coarsely grated

1 onion, finely grated

1 tbsp finely chopped fresh sage or 1 tsp dried sage

1 medium egg, lightly beaten

5 tbsps dried breadcrumbs

salt and black pepper

2 tbsp olive oil

Apple Sauce

315g tart cooking apples, peeled, cored and chopped

grated zest and juice of $\frac{1}{2}$ lemon

2 tbsps sugar or clear honey

1 tbsp finely chopped fresh sage or 1 tsp dried sage

4–5 tbsps sour cream (optional)

Puddings

1   Place the potatoes, parsnips, onion, sage, egg, breadcrumbs and seasoning in a large bowl and mix together well. Cover and place in the refrigerator for 20 minutes.

Apple Sauce

1   Place the apples, lemon zest and juice and sugar or honey in a small, heavy-based saucepan with 2 tablespoons of water. Bring to the boil, cover, then reduce the heat and cook for 8–10 minutes or until the mixture forms a chunky purée. Remove from the heat and stir for 1 minute or until fluffy. Add the sage and soured cream (if using).

2   Preheat the oven. Brush 6 Yorkshire pudding tins with $\frac{1}{2}$ the oil. Divide the pudding mixture between them, then brush the tops with $\frac{1}{2}$ the remaining oil and cook for 15 minutes. Remove from the oven, brush with the remaining oil and cook for 5 minutes longer or until browned. Serve with the apple sauce.

Serves 6

Oven temperature 220°C

Potato Feta Fritters

Preparation 20 mins + chilling **Cooking** 10 mins **Calories** 162 **Fat** 5g

1½ cups potato, mashed
120g feta cheese, crumbled
1 egg, beaten
3 spring onions, chopped
4 tbsps fresh dill, chopped, plus extra to garnish
1 tbsp lemon juice
zest of ½ a lemon, finely grated
freshly ground black pepper
plain flour, for dredging
olive oil
extra fresh dill and lemon zest, to garnish

1   In a medium bowl, add the potato, feta, egg, spring onions, dill, lemon juice, lemon zest and pepper. Mix until well combined. Cover and chill for 1–2 hours, until firm.

2   Using your hands, roll the mixture into 3cm patties and flatten them slightly. Dredge lightly in flour.

3   Heat a little oil in a frying pan, and cook a few at a time (until golden brown on both sides). Drain on a absorbent paper and serve immediately. Garnish with extra dill and lemon.

Serves 4

Sweet Potato and Rosemary Soup

Preparation 20 mins **Cooking** 1–1¼ hrs **Calories** 256 **Fat** 2g

40mL olive oil
2 cloves garlic, crushed
1 medium onion, chopped
3 tbsps rosemary, chopped
2 tbsps tomato pesto
1 medium carrot, diced
1 large potato, diced
680g sweet potato, diced
4 cups chicken stock
freshly ground pepper and salt

1 Heat the oil in a saucepan, add the garlic, onion and ⅓ of the rosemary, and cook on a medium heat for 3–5 minutes, or until soft.

2 Add the tomato pesto and cook for 1 minute.

3 Add the carrot, potato and sweet potato, and cook a further 5 minutes. Add the stock and pepper and salt, bring to the boil, reduce the heat, and simmer (with the lid on) for 30–40 minutes, or until the vegetables are soft.

4 Purée the soup in a food processor (you may have to do this in 2 batches), return the soup to the pan, add the remaining rosemary and heat through before serving. Add extra stock if the soup is too thick.

Serves 4–6

Sweet Potato and Cannellini Falafel

Preparation 30 mins **Cooking** 50 mins **Calories** 363 **Fat** 7g

Sweet Potato Falafel

400g orange sweet potato, cut into chunks

2 tsps olive oil

1 clove garlic, crushed

2 tsps ground cumin

1 tsp ground coriander

1 tbsp no-added-salt tomato paste

400g cooked or canned cannellini beans or chickpeas, rinsed and drained

2 tbsps chopped fresh coriander

1 tbsp tahini (sesame seed paste)

1 tbsp lemon juice

1 cup breadcrumbs, made from stale bread

6 large Lebanese or pita bread rounds

3 tbsps purchased or hummus

2 cups shredded lettuce

1 cup tabbouleh

1 red onion, thinly sliced

lemon juice, to taste

1. To make the falafel, boil or microwave the sweet potato until tender. Drain. Place in a bowl, mash and set aside.

2. Heat the oil in a non-stick frying pan over a medium heat. Add the garlic, cumin and ground coriander. Cook, stirring, for 1–2 minutes or until fragrant. Stir in the tomato paste. Cook for 3–4 minutes or until it becomes deep red and develops a rich aroma. Stir in the beans.

3. Place the mixture in a food processor. Add the fresh coriander, tahini and lemon juice. Using the pulse button, process to a coarse paste. Add this paste and the breadcrumbs to the mashed sweet potato. Mix to combine. Shape the mixture into 3cm patties. Roll in flour to coat. Place on a plate lined with plastic food wrap. Cover. Refrigerate for at least 30 minutes or until ready to cook – the patties can be made up to this stage a day in advance.

4. Preheat a barbecue or grill to a medium heat. Cook the falafel for 3–4 minutes each side or until golden and crispy.

5. Meanwhile, heat the bread on the barbecue grill. While still hot, spread the bread with hummus. Top with lettuce, tabbouleh and red onion. Place 3 falafel down 1 side of each bread round and squash slightly. Sprinkle with lemon juice to taste. Roll up tightly and serve immediately.

Serves 6

Salads

Potatoes are so versatile they can be used as a base for a whole array of tempting salads. They're also extremely nutritious, as the carbohydrate they contain gives a welcome energy boost. This chapter contains a range of delicious light meals which are ideal if you feel peckish rather than ravenous.

Potato Salad

Preparation 35 mins **Cooking** 40 mins **Calories** 492 **Fat** 8g

Salad

900g potatoes, peeled and cut into cubes

3 eggs

4 rashers bacon, rind removed, chopped

1 onion, finely chopped

2 spring onions, chopped

2 tbsps chopped fresh dill

1 tbsp chopped fresh mint

Mustard Dressing

1 cup mayonnaise

4 tbsps natural yogurt

1 tbsp Dijon mustard

freshly ground black pepper

1   Place the potatoes in a saucepan, cover with cold water and bring to the boil. Reduce the heat and simmer for 10–15 minutes or until the potatoes are tender. Drain and set aside to cool.

2   Place the eggs in a saucepan, cover with cold water and bring to the boil over a medium heat, then simmer for 10 minutes. Drain and cool under cold running water. Cool completely. Remove the shells and cut the eggs into quarters.

3   Place the bacon in a non-stick frying pan and cook over a medium heat, stirring occasionally, for 10 minutes or until crisp. Drain on absorbent paper.

4   Place the potatoes, eggs, bacon, onion, spring onions, dill and mint in a salad bowl and toss gently to combine.

Mustard Dressing

1   Combine the mayonnaise, yogurt, mustard and pepper to taste in a bowl. Spoon the dressing over the salad and toss to combine.

Serves 6

Curried Potato and Egg Salad

Preparation 10 mins **Cooking** 10 mins **Calories** 330 **Fat** 16g

750g potatoes
4 hard boiled eggs
¼ cup chopped chives
2 sticks celery
½ cup mayonnaise
3 tsps curry powder
1 tbsp finely chopped coriander

1. Peel potatoes and cut into cubes, then place in salted, boiling water. Cook until just tender. Drain well and place in a bowl.

2. Shell the eggs and chop roughly. Add to the potatoes and chives. Wash and trim celery, cut into thin slices and add to the potatoes.

3. Mix the mayonnaise and curry powder together and carefully mix through the potato mixture, taking care not to break up the potatoes. Serve garnished with chopped coriander.

Serves 4

Sweet Potato and Peanut Salad

Preparation 40 mins **Cooking** 1 hr **Calories** 588 **Fat** 4g

1¾ kg sweet potato, peeled

6 tbsps olive oil

20 cloves garlic, unpeeled

salt and pepper

1 Spanish onion, ground

1–2 small red chillies, ground

½ cup fresh herbs of your choice
(e.g. coriander, parsley, dill, chives or
a mixture)

2 tbsps balsamic vinegar

2 cups roasted peanuts

salt and freshly ground pepper

1 Cut the sweet potato into large chunks. Toss with 2 tablespoons of the oil and place in a large baking dish with the garlic. Season with salt and pepper and bake for about 1 hour or until the sweet potato is tender and golden around the edges. Remove from the oven and keep warm.

2 Mix the onion and chilli with the fresh herbs and combine with the sweet potato. Whisk the remaining olive oil with the vinegar and toss with the sweet potato mixture. Add the peanuts, toss again and serve. Season to taste, then garnish with extra herb sprigs.

Serves 8 as a side dish

Oven temperature 220°C

Sweet Potato Chip Salad

Preparation 40 mins **Cooking** 8–10 mins **Calories** 222 **Fat** 1g

900g sweet potatoes, thinly sliced
3–4 tbsps olive oil
170g baby English spinach leaves
170g rocket leaves
3 tomatoes, chopped
2 red onions, sliced
4 tbsps pitted black olives
55g Parmesan cheese shavings

Sweet Oregano Dressing
2 tbsps fresh oregano leaves
1½ tbsps brown sugar
⅓ cup balsamic vinegar
freshly ground black pepper

1   Preheat a barbecue to a high heat. Brush the sweet potatoes with oil and cook in batches on the barbecue plate (griddle) for 4 minutes each side or until golden and crisp. Drain on absorbent paper.

2   Place the spinach, rocket, tomatoes, onions, olives and cheese in a bowl and toss to combine. Cover and chill until required.

3   To make the dressing, place the oregano, sugar, vinegar and pepper to taste in a screwtop jar and shake to combine.

4   To serve, add the sweet potato chips to the salad, drizzle with the dressing and toss to combine.

Serves 8

Warm Herbed Potato Salad

Preparation 20 mins **Cooking** 40 mins **Calories** 352 **Fat** 3g

1⅓ kg Russet or Idaho potatoes
2 tbsps olive oil
4 white onions, sliced
¼ cup chopped fresh dill
¼ cup chopped fresh chervil
¼ cup chopped fresh parsley
zest of 1 lemon
salt and freshly ground pepper

Dressing
⅔ cup olive oil
4 tbsps white wine vinegar
juice of 1 lemon
3 cloves garlic

1 Cut the unpeeled (well washed) potatoes into large chunks and boil in salted water for 10 minutes or until tender but not soft. In a separate pan, heat the oil and sauté the onions over a high heat until golden, about 8 minutes. Reduce the heat, cover and cook slowly for 20 minutes.

2 Drain the potatoes and return to the saucepan.

3 In a jug, whisk the dressing ingredients until thickened. Pour the dressing over the hot potatoes and toss, adding the fresh herbs and lemon zest with salt and lots of pepper to taste.

4 Add the caramelised onions and toss thoroughly.

Serves 6–8

Provençal Salad of Potatoes, Beans and Roquefort *(not photographed)*

Preparation 35 mins **Cooking** 45 mins **Calories** 550 **Fat** 8g

2 tbsps white wine vinegar
juice of 1 lemon
145mL extra virgin olive oil
1–2 tbsps seeded mustard
salt and pepper, to taste
1⅓ kg small red potatoes, quartered
455g slender green beans
185g crumbled Roquefort cheese
½ cup walnuts, toasted and chopped
1 bunch of chives, coarsely snipped

1 Whisk the vinegar, lemon juice, olive oil, mustard and salt and pepper to make a thick and emulsified vinaigrette.

2 Toss the potatoes with 4 tablespoons of the vinaigrette until well coated. Transfer the potatoes to a baking dish and cook in a preheated oven for 40 minutes, or until tender and crisp around the edges.

3 Blanch the beans in salted boiling water until just tender, about 2 minutes, then immediately plunge into cold water to stop the cooking process. Toss with a little of the vinaigrette while still warm.

4 To serve, toss the warm potatoes, beans, cheese and a little extra vinaigrette together in a large bowl until the mixture is well combined.

5 Arrange on a platter, scatter the walnuts and chives on top and serve.

Serves 6–8

Oven temperature 220°C

Main Courses

This chapter contains a wide selection of delicious
main meal dishes which are more substantial than
the snack and light meal section and generally
require more preparation and cooking. The potato
is the main ingredient in the majority of these recipes,
but they also include ideas for adding meat, poultry,
fish and vegetarian ingredients – so there's
something for everyone.

Bean Cottage Pie

Preparation 20 mins **Cooking** 40 mins **Calories** 358 **Fat** 3g

1 tbsp vegetable oil

2 cloves garlic, crushed

2 leeks, white parts only, sliced

2 large carrots, sliced

400g canned tomatoes, undrained and mashed

400g canned lima or butter beans, drained

freshly ground black pepper

680g potatoes, cooked and mashed

55g grated aged Cheddar cheese

1. Heat the oil in a large frying pan, add the garlic, leeks and carrots and cook, stirring, for 5 minutes or until the leeks are tender. Add the tomatoes, bring to the boil, then reduce the heat and simmer for 10 minutes or until the mixture reduces and thickens.

2. Stir in the beans and cook for 3–4 minutes longer. Season to taste with pepper.

3. Transfer the bean mixture to a greased ovenproof dish, top with the mashed potato and sprinkle with the cheese. Bake in oven for 20 minutes or until the top is golden.

Serves 4

Oven temperature 200°C

Cheesy Baked Potato Rösti

Preparation 15 mins **Cooking** 30 mins **Calories** 181 **Fat** 10g

500g potatoes, peeled, grated and
squeezed dry
bunch of spring onions, chopped
25g butter, melted
salt and black pepper
1 tsp peanut oil
100g Gruyère cheese, grated

1 Preheat the oven. Place the potatoes and ⅔ of the spring onions in a bowl, add the butter and seasoning, then mix together well.

2 Heat the oil in an ovenproof frying pan. Place the potato mixture in the pan and press with the back of a spoon to make an even layer. Fry for 5–6 minutes, until the edges start to brown, then transfer to the oven and bake for 10 minutes or until the top has browned.

3 Increase the oven temperature to 230°C. Mix the cheese with the remaining spring onions. Remove the pan from the oven and sprinkle the cheese and onion mixture over the rösti. Return to the oven and bake for 6–8 minutes, until the cheese is bubbling and golden.

Serves 6

Oven temperature 200°C

Clapshot Pie

Preparation 20 mins **Cooking** 1 hr 55 mins **Calories** 397 **Fat** 21g

1 tbsp olive or sunflower oil
1 large onion, chopped
1 large carrot, finely chopped
55g bacon, chopped
¾ kg minced beef
1⅕ cups beef stock
2 tbsps tomato sauce
1 tbsp Worcestershire sauce
1 tsp chopped fresh thyme
salt and black pepper
2 tbsps chopped fresh parsley, plus extra to garnish

Topping
455g potatoes, chopped
455g swede, chopped
salt and black pepper
55g butter
145mL light cream
freshly grated nutmeg

1. Heat the oil in a frying pan, then fry the onion, carrot and bacon for 10 minutes or until browned. Add the beef and fry for 10–15 minutes, breaking up any lumps with the back of a wooden spoon, until the meat has browned. Spoon off any excess fat, then stir in the stock, sauces, thyme and seasoning. Simmer partly covered for 45 minutes, stirring occasionally, until thickened. Add a little water if the mixture becomes too dry.

2. Meanwhile, cook the potatoes and swede in boiling salted water for 15–20 minutes, until tender. Drain, then mash with ½ the butter and the cream. Season with pepper and nutmeg.

3. Preheat the oven. Transfer the beef to a 1½ litre shallow ovenproof dish, then stir in the parsley. Smooth over the potato and swede mixture, then fluff it up with a fork and dot with the remaining butter. Bake for 35–45 minutes, until browned. Garnish with parsley.

Serves 6

Note: Clapshot is the Scottish name for a mixture of mashed potato and swede, hence the name of this cottage pie.

Oven temperature 200°C

Cheese, Ham and Scalloped Potatoes *(not photographed)*

Preparation 30 mins **Cooking** 1 hr **Calories** 800 **Fat** 42g

1 kg potatoes, peeled and soaked in cold water
90g butter
2 large onions, sliced
1½ tsps sugar
250g fresh breadcrumbs, air dried for about 4 hours
375g shaved, smoked ham
250g Gruyere cheese
freshly ground black pepper, to taste
ground nutmeg, to taste
2 cups whipping cream, hot
4 tbsps fresh breadcrumbs
4 tbsps Parmesan cheese

1. Bring a large pot of water to the boil. Slice each potato into 1cm thick slices, and drop into the boiling water. Cook for about 5 minutes or until just slightly tender. Drain and completely dry on a clean kitchen towel.

2. Melt 60g of the butter in a large frying pan over medium heat. Sauté the onions until golden brown, adding the sugar after 3–4 minutes to caramelise the onions. Set aside. Fry the 250g bread crumbs in the remaining 30g butter until golden. Set aside. Heat the oven to 190°

3. Lightly butter a large oval baking dish. Layer in half the onions, potatoes, ham shavings, cheese and browned breadcrumbs, season with pepper and nutmeg. Repeat.

4. Cover the assembled dish with the hot cream, pouring it over slowly and evenly. Allow the cream to settle for 5 minutes. Sprinkle the top with the remaining 4 tablespoons breadcrumbs and Parmesan. Bake for 30–35 minutes until it is bubbly, the cream is absorbed and the top is a beautiful brown.

5. Remove from the oven and let stand for 20 minutes before serving to allow the sauce to thicken.

Serves 6

Chilli Bean Potatoes

Preparation 60–75 mins **Cooking** 20 mins **Calories** 215 **Fat** 2 g

4 potatoes, scrubbed
1 tbsp tomato purée
1–2 tsps hot chilli sauce, or to taste
285g canned red kidney beans, drained and rinsed
freshly ground black pepper
paprika

1   Bake the potatoes for 45–60 minutes or until soft. Remove from the oven and allow to cool slightly.

2   Cut the tops from the potatoes and scoop out the flesh, leaving a thin shell. Place the potato flesh, tomato purée and chilli sauce in a bowl and mash. Stir in the beans and season with pepper.

3   Spoon the potato mixture into the potato shells, dust with paprika and bake for 10–15 minutes or until heated through and lightly browned.

Serves 4

Oven temperature 220°C

Seared Salmon with Rosemary Sweet Potatoes

Preparation 15 mins **Cooking** 25 mins **Calories** 616 **Fat** 30g

680g sweet potatoes, cut into 1cm dice
2 cloves garlic, roughly chopped
1 tbsp chopped fresh rosemary, plus sprigs to garnish
4 tbsps olive oil, plus extra to serve
1 tbsp black peppercorns
4 salmon fillets, about 170g each
salt and black pepper
lemon wedges and fresh rosemary, to garnish

1 Toss the sweet potatoes with the garlic, rosemary and ½ the oil. Transfer to a small roasting tin and bake for 20 minutes, stirring halfway through, until softened. Crush the peppercorns using a mortar and pestle. Brush the salmon with the remaining oil, coat with the crushed peppercorns and season.

2 Heat a ridged cast-iron grill pan or heavy-based frying pan. Add the salmon, skin-side down, and cook for 4 minutes, then turn and cook for a further 1 minute, until cooked through. Cover with foil and set aside.

3 Spoon the potatoes and any pan juices onto plates and top with the salmon. Drizzle over a little olive oil and serve garnished with lemon wedges and rosemary.

Serves 4

Note: Garlic and rosemary-infused sweet potatoes served with salmon fillets make an inspired partnership. A drizzle of oil and a squeeze of lemon round things off perfectly.

Oven temperature 230°C

Gnocchi with Pork and Peppers

Preparation 20 mins + 1 hr marinating **Cooking** 35 mins **Calories** 638 **Fat** 26g

340g pork steak, cubed
4 cloves garlic, very finely chopped
1 tbsp dried oregano
juice of ½ lemon
6 tbsps extra virgin olive oil
salt and black pepper
2 tbsps very finely chopped onion
1 tbsp very finely chopped celery
3 tbsps very finely chopped
fresh parsley
255g yellow capsicum deseeded and
cut into 2½cm pieces
200mL tomato purée
3 tbsps beef stock
800g gnocchi
30g black olives, pitted and cut
into strips

1 Place the pork in a shallow, non-metallic dish and mix in ½ the garlic, the oregano and lemon juice, 1 tablespoon of the oil and the seasoning. Cover and place in the refrigerator to marinate for 1 hour.

2 Heat the remaining oil in a large heavy-based saucepan. Add the onion and a pinch of salt and fry for 5 minutes or until softened. Stir in the remaining garlic and the celery, parsley and capsicum and cook over a low heat for 10 minutes or until the capsicum begins to soften.

3 Mix in the tomato purée and simmer for 10 minutes, stirring often. Add the pork, marinade and the stock. Simmer uncovered, stirring occasionally, for 10 minutes or until the sauce has thickened and the pork is cooked.

4 Meanwhile, cook the gnocchi in plenty of boiling salted water until tender but still firm to the bite. Drain and transfer to a warmed bowl. Spoon over the sauce and toss, then scatter over the olives.

Serves 4

Note: Soft potato gnocchi, which are light, tiny dumplings, are brought to life by pork, capsicum and oregano.

Lancashire Hotpot

Preparation 20 mins **Cooking** 2 hrs 20 mins **Calories** 617 **Fat** 35g

45g butter or dripping
4 large lamb loin chops or
8 lamb cutlets, trimmed
¾ kg potatoes, thinly sliced
2 large onions, sliced
3 large carrots, sliced
salt and black pepper
2 cups lamb stock

1 Preheat the oven. Heat 30g of the butter or dripping in a frying pan and cook the chops or cutlets for 5 minutes each side to brown.

2 Arrange ½ the potatoes in a large casserole dish, and top with ½ the onions, then ½ the carrots – lightly seasoning each layer. Add the chops or cutlets and a final layer each of onions, carrots and potatoes, again seasoning each layer. Pour over the stock, then dot with the remaining butter or dripping.

3 Cover the casserole dish and bake for 30 minutes. Reduce the temperature to 150°C and bake for a further 1 hour. Increase the temperature to 200°C, then uncover the dish and cook for 30–40 minutes, until the potatoes have browned.

Serves 4

Note: Layers of potato, onions and carrots sandwich tender loin chops in this traditional hotpot. It's a meal in itself – all it needs is a glass of ale or cider to wash it down.

Oven temperature 200°C

Lemon-Scented Fish Pie

Preparation 20 mins **Cooking** 1 hr **Calories** 464 **Fat** 13g

1 kg potatoes, cut into even-sized pieces

55g butter

1 onion, chopped

2 sticks celery, sliced

2 tbsps plain flour

1 cup fish stock

finely grated zest and juice of 1 large lemon

salt and black pepper

455g cod loin, cut into cubes

170g cooked and shelled mussels

2 tbsps chopped fresh parsley

4 tbsps milk

1 Cook the potatoes in boiling salted water for 15–20 minutes, until tender, then drain.

2 Meanwhile, melt ½ the butter in a large saucepan, add the onion and celery and cook for 2–3 minutes, until softened. Add the flour and cook, stirring, for 1 minute, then slowly add the stock and cook, stirring, until thickened. Add the lemon zest and juice and season with pepper.

3 Preheat the oven. Remove the sauce from the heat, stir in the cod, mussels and parsley, then transfer to an ovenproof dish.

4 Mash the potatoes with the remaining butter and the milk. Season, then spread the potato evenly over the fish with a fork. Bake for 30–40 minutes, until the sauce is bubbling and the topping starts to brown.

Serves 4

Note: Creamy mashed potatoes make a wonderful topping for this pie. If you wish, replace the mussels with peeled prawns.

Oven temperature 220°C

Crab Stuffed Potatoes

Preparation 30 mins **Cooking** 20 mins **Calories** 311 **Fat** 8g

6 potatoes, baked
1 tbsp butter
115mL sour cream
55g onion, grated
¼ tsp pepper
125g crab meat, diced
55g mushrooms, diced
115g Cheddar cheese, grated

1 Bake potatoes for 45–60 minutes or until soft. Remove from the oven and allow to cool slightly.
2 Preheat the oven.
3 Cut the potatoes in half lengthwise and carefully scoop out the flesh, reserving the skins.
4 In a bowl, mash the potato flesh, then add the butter, sour cream, onion and pepper. Beat until smooth. Fold in the crab meat and mushrooms and place the mixture back in the 12 potato skin halves. Sprinkle with the cheese and place on a baking tray.
5 Bake for 15–20 minutes, or until the potatoes are heated through.

Serves 6

Oven temperature 200°C

Warm Barbecued Octopus and Potato Salad

Preparation 25 mins + marinating **Cooking** 5 mins **Calories** 202 **Fat** 8g

455g baby octopus, cleaned

455g pink-skinned potatoes
(e.g. Russet or Idaho), washed

rocket or mixed salad greens

2 Lebanese cucumbers, chopped

2 green onions, finely sliced

Lime and Chilli Marinade

2 tbsps olive oil

juice of 1 lime or lemon

1 fresh red chilli, diced

1 clove garlic, crushed

Tomato Concasse (optional)

4 plum tomatoes, diced

½ cup chopped fresh coriander

½ red onion, diced

⅓ cup balsamic or sherry vinegar

1 tbsp olive oil

1 tbsp lemon juice

freshly ground black pepper

1 To make the marinade, place the oil, lime or lemon juice, chilli and garlic in a bowl and mix to combine.

2 Cut the octopus in half lengthwise (if very small, leave whole) and add it to the marinade. Marinate in the refrigerator for at least 2 hours or overnight.

3 Boil or microwave the potatoes until tender. Drain. Cool slightly. Cut into bite-size chunks.

4 To make the concasse, place the tomatoes, coriander, onion, vinegar, oil, lemon juice and pepper to taste in a bowl. Mix to combine.

5 Preheat a barbecue plate or char-grill pan to very hot.

6 Line a serving platter with the rocket or mixed greens. Top with the potatoes, cucumbers and onions.

7 Drain the octopus. Cook on the barbecue or char-grill, turning frequently, for 3–5 minutes or until the tentacles curl. Take care not to overcook or the octopus or it will become tough.

8 To serve, spoon the hot octopus over the prepared salad. Top with concasse (if using). Accompany with crusty bread.

Serves 6

Tuna Potato Roulade *(not photographed)*

Preparation 10 mins **Cooking** 10 mins **Calories** 650 **Fat** 6g

1 kg potatoes, peeled

100g spring onions, chopped (white part only)

3 cups wholemeal breadcrumbs

1 egg white

plain flour

Filling

200g can tuna (water packed)

200g spring onions, chopped (green part only)

1 apple, peeled and cut into quarters

10 medium field mushrooms, washed

1 tbsp lemon juice

1 Boil potatoes until tender, drain and mash. Fold in white spring onions, breadcrumbs and egg white and mix well.

2 Place a sheet of foil over a 30 x 33cm baking tray. Sprinkle over plain flour. Whilst potato is still warm, spoon it in blobs over the baking tray. Flatten with your hand until it covers the tray about 1cm thick.

3 Lightly blend the filling in a food processor. Spoon this mixture along one edge of the longest side of the foil, press down firmly. Pick up the end of the foil at the same edge and begin to roll over (if filling starts to fall out, just keep pressing it back into position with your hand). Roll until there is no more potato. Use a knife or spatula to flatten edge on to the main roll to make an even finish.

4 Place carefully on a lightly greased baking tray. Cook in a hot oven at 250°C for 30 minutes. Reduce heat and cook for a further 30 minutes at 200°C. Serve with lightly steamed seasonal vegetables.

Serves 6

Potato, Cheese and Onion Pie

Preparation 30 mins + 10 mins cooling **Cooking** 1 hr 15 mins **Calories** 910 **Fat** 62g

455g fresh shortcrust pastry
455g waxy potatoes, very thinly sliced
1 small onion, very thinly sliced
100g Red Leicester (or hard cheese), finely grated
salt and black pepper
145mL cream

1   Preheat the oven. Roll ⅔ of the pastry on to a lightly floured work surface and use it to line a 23cm flan dish. Arrange the potatoes in a single layer over the base of the dish, then top with a layer each of the onion and cheese, seasoning well between each layer. Pour over the cream.

2   Roll out the remaining pastry to make a lid. Lightly dampen the edges of the pie with water. Place the pastry lid on top and pinch the edges together to seal well.

3   Bake for 1–1¼ hours, until the potatoes and onions are tender. Leave for 10 minutes before serving to allow the cheese to cool slightly.

Serves 4

Note: Waxy potatoes are best for this recipe as they hold their shape well. Serve the pie hot with lightly steamed savoy cabbage or cold with a crisp salad.

Oven temperature 180°C

Potato Omelette

Preparation 35 mins **Cooking** 5–10 mins **Calories** 470 **Fat** 6g

5 eggs
1 cup olive oil
1 kg potatoes, peeled and thinly sliced
1 small onion, peeled (optional)
salt

1 Beat the egg in a bowl.

2 Heat the oil in a frying pan, add the potatoes and onion, season and cover. Fry gently, moving the pan to prevent sticking. Once the potatoes are cooked (take care they don't become crisp) break them up, remove them from the pan with a slotted spoon and add them to the eggs. Stir the potatoes until well covered with egg. Add salt to taste.

3 Remove all but a tablespoon of the oil from the frying pan, Heat the oil, return the egg and potato mixture to the pan and cook for a few minutes until one side is golden.

4 Next (this is slightly tricky), slip the omelette, cooked side down, onto a plate slightly larger than the pan. Then slip it back into the pan, cooked side up. Cook until firm.

5 Your omelette should be about 3.5cm thick. If you're using it for tapas, cut it into squares.

Serves 6–8 as a side dish

Rich Fish Stew on Rosemary Mash

Preparation 40 mins **Cooking** 20–30 mins **Calories** 304 **Fat** 2g

Stew

2 tsps olive oil
1 leek, chopped
1 clove garlic, crushed
1 tsp ground oregano
4 flat mushrooms, sliced
1 stalk celery, sliced
1 tbsp no-added-salt tomato paste
2 zucchini, sliced
400g canned no-added-salt diced tomatoes
½ cup dry white wine
455g firm white fish fillets (e.g. gemfish, ling, barramundi, sea bass or blue-eye cod)
1 tbsp chopped fresh basil
1 tbsp chopped fresh parsley

Rosemary Mash

1 sprig fresh rosemary
2 tsp olive oil
2 large potatoes, chopped
¼ cup low-fat milk, warmed
ground white pepper
lemon juice (optional)
rosemary sprigs, for garnish

Rosemary Mash

1. Remove the leaves from the rosemary sprig. Place the leaves and oil in a small saucepan over a low heat. Heat until warm. Remove the pan from the heat and set aside to let the flavours to develop. If possible, do this several hours in advance; the longer the leaves steep in the oil, the more pronounced the flavour.

2. Boil or microwave the potatoes until tender. Drain well. Add the milk and rosemary oil. Mash. Season with pepper and lemon juice to taste. Keep warm or reheat just before serving.

Stew

1. Heat the oil in a large deep-sided non-stick frying pan over a medium heat. Add the leek and garlic. Cook, stirring, for 1–2 minutes or until soft. Add the oregano, mushrooms and celery. Cook, stirring, for 2–3 minutes. Stir in the tomato paste. Cook for 3–4 minutes or until it becomes deep red and develops a rich aroma.

2. Stir in the zucchini, tomatoes and wine. Bring to the boil. Reduce the heat. Simmer, stirring occasionally, for 5 minutes or until the mixture starts to thicken.

3. Add the fish. Cook for 6 minutes or until fish is just cooked – take care not to overcook or the fish will fall apart. Stir in the basil and parsley.

4. To serve, place a mound of mash on each serving plate. Top with fish stew. Accompany with a green salad or steamed green vegetables of your choice. Garnish with rosemary sprigs.

Serves 4

Root Vegetable Curry

Preparation 20 mins **Cooking** 55 mins **Calories** 219 **Fat** 4g

1 tbsp olive oil

1 onion, chopped

1 green chilli, deseeded and chopped

1 clove garlic, finely chopped

2½cm piece fresh root ginger, finely chopped

2 tbsps plain flour

2 tsps each ground coriander, ground cumin and turmeric

1⅕ cups vegetable stock

200mL tomato purée

750g mixed root vegetables, such as potato, sweet potato, celeriac and swede, diced

2 carrots, thinly sliced

black pepper

chopped fresh coriander, to garnish

1 Heat the oil in a large saucepan. Add the onion, chilli, garlic and ginger and cook, stirring occasionally for 5 minutes or until softened. Stir in the flour, coriander, cumin and turmeric and cook gently, stirring, for 1 minute to release the flavours.

2 Gradually stir in the stock, then add the tomato purée, diced root vegetables and carrots. Season with pepper and mix well.

3 Bring to the boil, stirring, then cover, reduce the heat and simmer, stirring occasionally for 45 minutes or until the vegetables are tender. Garnish with coriander.

Serves 4

Note: This spicy curry is based on a traditional Moroccan dish. So, as a change from boiled rice, try serving it with hot fluffy couscous.

Salmon and Potato Lasagne

Preparation 40 mins **Cooking** 60–75 mins **Calories** 284 **Fat** 7g

Lasagne

1 tsp olive oil

1 onion, diced

2 stalks celery, diced

1 tbsp no-added-salt tomato paste

225g canned no-added-salt red or pink salmon, rinsed, drained and roughly mashed (don't remove the bones, they're full of calcium)

1 tbsp chopped fresh tarragon or 1 tsp dried tarragon

1⅕ cups low-fat milk

3 eggs, lightly beaten

2 egg whites, lightly beaten

juice of ½ lemon

freshly ground black pepper

4 large potatoes, thinly sliced

4 cups firmly packed English spinach leaves, blanched and squeezed to remove excess moisture

Breadcrumb and Parmesan Topping

½ cup breadcrumbs, made from stale bread

2 tbsps chopped fresh parsley

1 tbsp grated Parmesan cheese

Breadcrumb and Parmesan Topping

1   Place the breadcrumbs, parsley and cheese in a small bowl. Mix to combine. Set aside.

Lasagne

1   Preheat the oven. Lightly spray or brush a large flat casserole dish with unsaturated oil.

2   Heat the oil in a non-stick frying pan over a medium heat. Add the onion and celery. Cook, stirring, for 3-4 minutes or until soft. Stir in the tomato paste. Cook for 3–4 minutes or until it becomes deep red and develops a rich aroma. Transfer the mixture to a large bowl. Cool.

3   Add the salmon, tarragon, milk, eggs, egg whites, lemon juice and pepper to taste to the onion mixture. Mix to combine. Arrange ½ the potatoes over the base of the prepared dish. Pour over the salmon mixture. Top with the spinach. Cover with the remaining potatoes. Sprinkle with the topping. Bake for 1 hour or until the potatoes are tender and the mixture is set.

Serves 4

Oven temperature 180°C

Shepherd's Pie

Preparation 20 mins **Cooking** 40 mins **Calories** 522 **Fat** 20g

680g potatoes, peeled and cut into
even-sized chunks

salt and black pepper

2 tbsps vegetable oil

1 medium onion, chopped

1 stick celery, diced

1 medium carrot, diced

455g minced lamb

1 tbsp tomato purée

2 tbsps Worcestershire sauce

170mL lamb stock made with
½ stock cube

30g butter

55mL full-fat milk

1 Put the potatoes into a saucepan, cover with cold water and add ½ teaspoon of salt. Boil for 20 minutes or until tender.

2 Meanwhile, preheat the oven. Heat the oil in a large, heavy-based frying pan over a medium heat, then fry the onion, celery and carrot for 2–3 minutes, until softened.

3 Add the lamb to the pan, breaking it up with the back of a wooden spoon. Cook for 5 minutes or until browned, stirring all the time. Stir in the tomato purée and Worcestershire sauce, mixing well. Cook for 2 minutes. Add the stock, stir, season with salt and pepper, then simmer for 5 minutes.

4 Meanwhile, drain the potatoes and return them to the pan. Add the butter and milk, then mash with a potato masher or fork, until smooth.

5 Spoon the lamb mixture into a deep ovenproof dish, about 15 x 23cm. Top with the mashed potatoes, spreading them evenly and fluffing up the surface with a fork. Cook for 20 minutes or until the top is golden brown.

Serves 4

Oven temperature 200°C

Tortilla with Corn and Sun-Dried Tomatoes

Preparation 15 mins **Cooking** 20 mins **Calories** 324 **Fat** 23g

225g potatoes, thickly sliced
3 tbsps olive oil
3 tbsps canned corn, drained
4 sun-dried tomatoes in oil, drained and chopped
2 tbsps chopped fresh parsley
6 medium eggs, beaten
salt and black pepper

1 Boil the potatoes for 10 minutes and leave to cool slightly. Heat the oil in a large, flameproof, heavy-based frying pan, add the potato and fry over a high heat for 2–3 minutes, until browned and crisp. Reduce the heat, then stir in the corn and tomatoes and heat through for 1–2 minutes.

2 Preheat the grill to medium. In a bowl, add the parsley to the eggs and season, then pour over the vegetables in the frying pan. Cook over a low heat for 3–4 minutes, until the omelette base is set and lightly browned.

3 Place the pan under the grill for 1–2 minutes, until the top is set and golden. Leave to cool slightly, then cut into 4 wedges and serve with salad.

Serves 4

Salmon with Champ and Tomato Salad

Preparation 20 mins **Cooking** 30 mins **Calories** 702 **Fat** 42g

Salmon

55g fresh white breadcrumbs

6 tbsps chopped fresh basil, plus extra leaves to garnish

2 tbsps snipped fresh chives

5 tbsps olive oil

finely grated zest and juice of ½ lime

salt and black pepper

4 salmon fillets, about 170g each

200g cherry tomatoes, halved

Champ

750g potatoes, cut into even-sized chunks

salt and black pepper

200mL half-fat milk

45g butter

bunch of spring onions, chopped

Champ

1 Cook the potatoes in boiling salted water for 15 minutes or until tender. Place the milk, butter and all but 2 tablespoons of the spring onions in another saucepan and heat to just below boiling point. Drain and mash the potatoes, then stir in the milk mixture and season. Keep warm.

Salmon

1 Preheat the oven. Mix the breadcrumbs with ½ the basil and ½ the chives. Add 3 tablespoons of oil, the lime zest and seasoning. Place the salmon on a baking sheet and press the breadcrumb mixture onto the top and sides. Bake for 15 minutes or until the top is golden and the salmon is cooked.

2 While the salmon is cooking, whisk the remaining 2 tablespoon of oil with 1 tablespoon of lime juice in a bowl, then add the tomatoes, the reserved spring onions and the remaining basil and chives. Season to taste. Serve this tomato salad with the salmon and champ, garnished with basil.

Serves 4

Note: Champ, or Irish mash, goes particularly well with this herb-crusted salmon.

Oven temperature 200°C

Smoked Haddock Stew with Leek and Bacon

Preparation 20 mins + 10 mins standing **Cooking** 35 mins **Calories** 572 **Fat** 33g

3 cups full-fat milk

2 bay leaves

3 leeks, 1 cut in half lengthways, 2 thickly sliced

455g smoked haddock fillet

30g butter

115g rindless dry-cured smoked lean bacon, cut into 4cm wide strips

455g potatoes, cut into 3cm chunks

salt and black pepper

140mL light cream

lemon juice (optional)

2 tbsps chopped fresh parsley

2 tbsps snipped fresh chives, to garnish

1 Place the milk, bay leaves, halved leek and haddock in a saucepan. Bring to the boil, then simmer for 2–3 minutes. Cover the pan and set aside for 10 minutes. Remove the haddock, discard any skin and bones, flake the flesh and set aside. Discard the leek, but reserve the milk and bay leaves.

2 Heat the butter in a large heavy-based frying pan and fry the bacon for 2–3 minutes, until its fat starts to melt. Add the sliced leeks and cook for 5 minutes or until softened. Add the potatoes and cook for 3–4 minutes until slightly softened .

3 Add the reserved milk and bay leaves and $\frac{3}{5}$ cup of water. Season, bring to the boil, then cover and simmer for 15 minutes. Discard the bay leaves. Blend $\frac{1}{2}$ the mixture with $\frac{1}{2}$ the haddock using a hand blender, or mash with a potato masher. Return to the pan. Stir in the remaining haddock and the cream and reheat gently. Season and add lemon juice to taste, if using. Stir in the parsley. Sprinkle with chives.

Serves 4

Note: *This stew has a wonderfully rich, smoky flavour. Served with chunks of warm soda bread, it's a really satisfying meal.*

Tuna, Potato and Spring Onion Fish Cakes

Preparation 15 mins + 30 mins cooling **Cooking** 40 mins **Calories** 681 **Fat** 36g

4 slices bread, crusts removed

680g floury potatoes, such as Idaho, halved or quartered (depending on size)

salt

4 tbsps mayonnaise

400g can tuna in oil, drained and flaked

1 tbsp chopped fresh parsley

2 spring onions, finely chopped

finely grated zest of ½ small lemon

4 tbsps plain flour

1 medium egg, beaten

vegetable oil for frying

lemon wedges, to serve (optional)

1 Preheat the oven. Place the bread on a baking sheet and cook at the bottom of the oven for 20–30 minutes, until crisp. Cool, then break into pieces and crush with a rolling pin.

2 Meanwhile, cook the potatoes in a large saucepan of boiling salted water for 15 minutes or until tender. Drain, transfer to a bowl and mash with the mayonnaise. Leave to cool for 30 minutes.

3 Mash the tuna, parsley, spring onions and lemon zest into the potatoes. Flour your hands, then shape the mixture into 8 flat cakes. Dust them with flour and dip them into the egg, then into the breadcrumbs.

4 Heat 5mm of oil in a large heavy-based frying pan and cook the fish cakes for 3–4 minutes each side, until crisp and golden (you may have to cook them in batches). Drain on absorbent paper, then serve with the lemon wedges, if using.

Serves 4

Note: These chunky fish cakes are packed with flavour and it only takes a few vegetables or a salad to make a complete meal. Canned salmon works just as well as tuna.

Oven temperature 160°C

Rookery Cookery

Preparation 20 mins **Cooking** 20 mins **Calories** 369 **Fat** 15g

sunflower oil for greasing and frying
145g skinless boneless chicken breast, minced
2 tbsps fresh breadcrumbs
1 tbsp chopped fresh parsley
1 tsp dried thyme
1 tsp brown sauce
2 medium eggs, beaten
black pepper
225g waxy potatoes, peeled and grated
1 small onion, finely chopped

Sauce

1 tbsp crème fraîche
½ tsp mild mustard
2 tsps snipped fresh chives

1   To make the sauce, combine the crème fraîche, mustard and chives, then cover and refrigerate.

2   Preheat the grill to high. Cover the grill pan rack with foil and lightly grease. Mix together the chicken, breadcrumbs, parsley, thyme, brown sauce and ½ the beaten egg, then season. Shape the mixture into 8 'eggs', using your hands. Grill for 5–10 minutes, turning, until browned.

3   Meanwhile, make the nests. Place the grated potato in a tea towel and squeeze out any excess water. Put it into a bowl with the onion, stir in the rest of the beaten egg and season. Divide the mixture in half, shape into rounds and press to flatten slightly.

4   Heat a little oil in a large, heavy-based frying pan. Cook the rounds for 5–6 minutes each side, until golden.

5   Make a hollow in the centre of each nest, drain them on absorbent paper, then place them on plates. Spoon over the sauce, then top each nest with 4 eggs.

Serves 2

Note: Hatch a surprise for the kids with these golden, crunchy potato nests, topped with a creamy sauce and filled with four delicious bird's eggs.

West Indian Sweet Potato Risotto with Spiced Sour Cream

Preparation 40 mins **Cooking** 40 mins **Calories** 547 **Fat** 4g

900g sweet potato
455g butternut pumpkin
2 tbsps olive oil
2 onions, finely chopped
1 carrot, finely chopped
2 stalks celery, finely chopped
2 cloves garlic, ground
1 tsp green curry paste
400g arborio rice
⁴/₅ cup white wine
2 bay leaves
3 cups chicken stock
145mL sour or thickened cream
¼ tsp cinnamon
¼ tsp ground coriander
¼ tsp ground cumin
½ bunch chives, finely chopped

1 Peel and chop the sweet potato and pumpkin, reserving 200g of each and slicing it into matchsticks for later. Place the remainder in a saucepan and cover with water. Bring to the boil and simmer for 30 minutes until both vegetables are tender.

2 Drain, mash and set aside. In a large saucepan, heat the oil and add the onions, carrot, celery, garlic, curry paste and reserved raw pumpkin and sweet potato and sauté until the onions are softened, about 10 minutes.

3 Add the rice and stir to coat, making sure all the grains have a shiny surface and appear opaque. Add the wine and allow the liquid to be absorbed while the alcohol is evaporated. Add the bay leaves, mashed pumpkin/sweet potato mixture and ladle of stock. Stir the risotto vigorously while allowing the liquid to be absorbed, and when the mixture becomes dry, add the next addition of stock. Continue in this way until all the stock has been incorporated, then remove the saucepan from the heat.

4 In a small bowl, whisk the cream with the spices. To serve, remove the bay leaves, then mound the risotto in individual bowls and garnish with a generous dollop of spiced cream and a shower of chopped chives.

Serves 6–8

Roast Lamb Hash with Potato Pancakes

Potato Pancakes: **Preparation** 25 mins **Cooking** 10–15 mins **Calories** 384 **Fat** 4g
Roast Lamb Hash: **Preparation** 15 mins **Cooking** 20 mins **Calories** 384 **Fat** 10g

Potato Pancakes

200g potatoes, scrubbed and grated

200g white sweet potatoes, peeled and grated

200g orange sweet potatoes, peeled and grated

1 red onion, finely chopped

2 tbsps plain flour

2 tbsps chopped fresh parsley or basil

1 tbsp grated Parmesan cheese

2 eggs, lightly beaten

freshly ground black pepper

Roast Lamb Hash

1 tsp unsaturated oil

1 small onion, diced

1 stalk celery, chopped

2 tbsps no-added-salt tomato paste

400g lean roast lamb, cut into bite-size cubes

425g canned no-added-salt diced tomatoes

2 tbsps chopped fresh parsley or basil

freshly ground black pepper

Potato Pancakes

1. Place the potatoes, sweet potatoes, onion, flour, parsley or basil, cheese, eggs and pepper to taste in a bowl. Mix to combine.

2. Lightly spray or brush a non-stick frying pan with olive oil. Heat over a high heat. Take 2–3 tablespoons of the mixture and place in the pan. Press down slightly to form pancakes. Cook for 4–5 minutes each side or until golden. Remove to a baking dish, lined with absorbent paper. Keep warm in a low oven. Repeat with the remaining mixture. Cook 3–4 pancakes at a time or as many as will fit in the pan.

3. Serve with the roast lamb hash, fresh tomato sauce and a green salad.

Serves 4

Note: These pancakes are an adaptation of the traditional latkes. You can also use the mixture to make a dish similar to a rosti by making one large pancake and finishing it under the grill. If you don't have time to stand over the frying pan, place mounds of mixture on a greased baking tray and bake at 180°C for 15 minutes. Turn over and cook for 8 minutes longer.

Roast Lamb Hash

1. Heat the oil in a saucepan over a medium heat. Add the onion and celery. Cook, stirring, for 2–3 minutes or until soft.

2. Stir in the tomato paste and cook for 3–4 minutes or until it turns deep red and develops a rich aroma.

3. Add the lamb, tomatoes, parsley or basil and pepper to taste. Cook, stirring occasionally, for 5–10 minutes or until the meat is heated and the sauce reduces and thickens.

4. Serve with the potato pancakes.

Serves 4

Note: This is a very simple home-style comfort dish. If you want to jazz it up a bit, you might like to add some chopped artichoke hearts, semi-dried tomatoes, roasted peppers or other gourmet vegetables and maybe a splash of wine. It's also delicious served with plain mashed potato.

Jack and the Bean Pork

Preparation 15 mins **Cooking** 35 mins **Calories** 472 **Fat** 22g

225g potatoes, diced
1 small carrot, diced
knob of butter
black pepper
1 tsp vegetable oil
3 spring onions, chopped
1 small clove garlic, crushed
8 cocktail sausages or 4 pork sausages, halved widthways
200g canned ratatouille
115g canned mixed beans, rinsed and drained
30g Cheddar, grated
thin strips of zucchini
14 whole snow peas

1 Cook the potatoes and carrot in boiling water for 10–15 minutes, until tender, then drain well and mash with the butter and pepper.

2 Heat the oil in a saucepan. Fry the spring onions and garlic for 3 minutes or until softened. Add the sausages and cook for 10–15 minutes, until browned and cooked through. Stir in the ratatouille and beans and heat through, then season again.

3 Preheat the grill to medium. Transfer the sausage mixture to a flameproof dish, top with the mash and sprinkle with cheese. Grill for 3 minutes or until the cheese browns. Meanwhile, cook the zucchini and snow peas in boiling water for 2 minutes to soften. Arrange the zucchini on top of the pie in the shape of a beanstalk, using the snow peas as leaves.

Serves 2

Note: This nutritious dish will transport children to the fairytale world of giants. Perhaps the beans are magic!

Moroccan Potato and Lemon Casserole

Preparation 20 mins **Cooking** 45 mins **Calories** 368 **Fat** 16g

3 tbsps olive oil
2 onions, sliced
3 cloves garlic, chopped
2 red chillies, finely chopped
1 tsp ground cumin
1 tsp ground coriander
900g waxy potatoes, cut into 5mm slices
grated rind of 1 lemon, and juice of 1–2 lemons
4 cups vegetable stock
salt and black pepper
4 tbsps sour cream, to serve
3 tbsps chopped fresh parsley, to garnish

1 Preheat the oven. Heat the oil in a flameproof and ovenproof casserole dish. Add the onions, garlic, chillies, cumin and coriander, then gently fry for 1–2 minutes to release their flavours.

2 Stir in the potatoes, lemon zest and juice to taste, then add the stock and seasoning. Bring to the boil, cover, then bake in the oven for 40 minutes or until the vegetables are tender and the liquid has reduced slightly.

3 Transfer to plates and top each serving with a spoonful of sour cream. Sprinkle over fresh parsley to garnish.

Serves 4

Oven temperature 200°C

Side Dishes

When the potato is thought of as a component of a meal, it's generally associated with meat and vegetables, served either roasted or boiled.
In fact, the potato is so easily combined with other flavours and able to be cooked in so many different ways, it's the perfect base for a variety of delicious side dishes. This chapter demonstrates that versatility with a wide range of tantalising recipes.

Scalloped Potatoes and Peaches

Preparation 40 mins **Cooking** 60–75 mins **Calories** 251 **Fat** 5g

4 medium potatoes, washed and peeled

salt and pepper

¼ tsp nutmeg

1 cup grated cheese

200g dried peaches

¾ cup cream or half milk/half cream

fresh sage, to garnish

1 Butter a large casserole dish. Slice the potatoes thinly. Mix the salt, pepper, nutmeg and cheese together. Place a layer of potatoes in base of casserole dish and sprinkle with 1 tablespoon of cheese mixture. Repeat with a second layer.

2 Place a layer of peaches over the potatoes and continue with 2 layers of potatoes and cheese mixture and 1 layer of peaches until all ingredients are used. Finish with a potato and cheese layer.

3 Pour in the cream. Cover with a lid or foil. Place in a preheated oven and cook for 1–1¼ hours, until the potato is tender. Remove the lid or foil for the last 15 minutes of cooking to brown the top. Serve as an accompaniment to meat, chicken or fish. Garnish with fresh sage.

Serves 6–8

Oven temperature 180°C

Sweet Potato and Onion Layered Bake

Preparation 10 mins **Cooking** 1 hr 5 mins **Calories** 210 **Fat** 8g

3 tbsps olive oil
3 onions, sliced into thin rings
750g sweet potatoes, thinly sliced
salt and black pepper
³⁄₅ cup chicken or vegetable stock

1 Preheat the oven. Heat ½ the oil in a wok or large, heavy-based frying pan. Add the onions and fry for 8–10 minutes, until golden brown.

2 Arrange ⅓ of the sweet potatoes in an ovenproof dish and top with ½ the onions. Season and cover with another layer of sweet potato. Cover with the remaining onions, season, then finish with a final layer of sweet potato.

3 Pour over the stock, cover the dish with foil and bake for 40–45 minutes, until the potatoes are just tender. Remove the foil and drizzle with the remaining oil. Increase the oven temperature to 230°C and bake for a further 8–10 minutes, until most of the liquid has evaporated and the top has browned.

Serves 6

Oven temperature 200°C

Sweet Potato Purée

Preparation 10 mins **Cooking** 15 mins **Calories** 200 **Fat** 3g

750g sweet potatoes, cut into large chunks
4 tbsps full-fat milk
1 clove garlic, crushed
45g half-fat aged Cheddar, finely grated
1 tbsp chopped fresh parsley
1 tbsp snipped fresh chives, plus extra to garnish
black pepper

1 Cook the sweet potatoes in a saucepan of boiling water for 10–15 minutes, until tender. Drain thoroughly, then mash until very smooth.

2 Heat the milk in a saucepan, then add it to the potato with the garlic, Cheddar, parsley, chives and pepper. Beat until smooth and well mixed, then serve hot, garnished with the chives.

Serves 4

Note: Strictly speaking, this is a side dish but the cheese and herbs make it so good you may not want to eat anything else other than some warm bread and a salad.

Mustard Scalloped Potatoes *(not photographed)*

Preparation 25 mins **Cooking** 1 hour 45 mins **Calories** 530 **Fat** 40g

1 cup cream
1 tbsp Dijon mustard
2 tbsps chopped fresh chives
¼ tsp salt
¼ tsp freshly ground black pepper
3 tbsps butter, softened
1 large garlic clove, crushed
750g potatoes, peeled and sliced thinly
1 large onion, sliced thinly
250g grated Parmesan cheese

1 Heat oven to 180°C

2 In a small bowl, blend together the cream and mustard. Stir in chives, salt and pepper.

3 In another small, bowl beat together the butter and garlic.

4 Arrange a quarter of the potato slices in overlapping layers in a lightly buttered 2 litre casserole dish. Dot with a quarter of the garlic butter. Layer on a third of the onion slices and sprinkle with a third of the cheese. Repeat, layering twice more and finishing with an overlapping layer of potatoes. Dot with the remaining garlic butter and pour the cream mixture over the top.

5 Bake, covered, for 1 hour. Remove the cover and bake 30–45 minutes longer, until the potatoes are cooked and the top is golden brown.

Serves 6

Note: Do not prepare this dish too far in advance of cooking, as the potatoes may discolour.

Potato and Onion Dauphinoise

Preparation 15 mins **Cooking** 1 hr **Calories** 425 **Fat** 24g

2 tsps butter, plus extra for greasing
680g baking potatoes
3 onions, thinly sliced
salt and black pepper
1 tsp freshly grated nutmeg
2 cups single cream

1 Preheat the oven. Butter a shallow ovenproof dish. Thinly slice the potatoes using the slicing blade on a food processor, or with a sharp knife.

2 Arrange the potatoes and onions in alternate layers in the dish, lightly seasoning each layer with salt, pepper and nutmeg. Finish with a potato layer, then pour over the cream and dot with butter. Place on the lower shelf of the oven and cook for 1 hour or until golden brown.

Serves 4

Note: The cream seeps into the layers of potato and onion in this wonderfully rich French gratin. Treat your friends to it on a special occasion.

Oven temperature 180°C

Garlic and Potato Mash

Preparation 15 mins **Cooking** 25 mins **Calories** 385 **Fat** 16g

1 kg large potatoes, cut into chunks

salt and black pepper

4 tbsps olive oil

2 heads of garlic, cloves separated and peeled

1 red onion, chopped

3 tbsps crème fraîche

4 tbsps snipped fresh chives

1 Put the potatoes into a large saucepan of lightly salted boiling water, bring back to the boil, then simmer for 15–20 minutes, until tender.

2 Meanwhile, heat the oil in a heavy-based frying pan or saucepan over a low to medium heat. Add the garlic, cover the pan and cook gently for 10–15 minutes, until tender and golden at the edges. Remove the garlic and set aside. Add the onion to the oil and cook for 10 minutes or until softened.

3 Drain the potatoes, then return them to the pan and add the garlic, onion and oil. Mash well, stir in the crème fraîche and chives and season to taste.

Serves 4

Potato Gratin

Preparation 25 mins **Cooking** 45 mins **Calories** 342 **Fat** 11g

900g potatoes, thinly sliced
2 large onions, thinly sliced
2 tbsps snipped fresh chives
freshly ground black pepper
1¼ cups low-fat natural yogurt
1 cup double cream
55g grated Parmesan cheese

1 Layer the potatoes, onions, chives and pepper to taste in 6 lightly greased individual ovenproof dishes.

2 Place the yogurt and cream in a bowl and mix to combine. Carefully pour the yogurt mixture over the potatoes and sprinkle with the cheese. Bake for 45 minutes or until the potatoes are tender and the top is golden.

Serves 6

Fried Potatoes

Preparation 30 mins **Cooking** 10 mins **Calories** 279 **Fat** 4g

1½ tbsp butter

3 tbsps olive oil

4 potatoes, peeled and cut into 7½mm slices

salt and pepper

chopped parsley

1 Heat the butter and oil together in a large pan. Fry the potatoes until tender and browned on both sides. Drain on absorbent paper.

2 Place on a serving plate and sprinkle with salt, pepper and parsley.

Serves 4

Baby New Potatoes with Lemon and Olives

Preparation 10 mins **Cooking** 30 mins **Calories** 228 **Fat** 11g

1 lemon
750g baby new potatoes, halved if large
2 cloves garlic, sliced
2 tbsps olive oil
salt and black pepper
1 tbsp butter
45g pitted green olives, quartered

1   Preheat the oven. Halve the lemon. Squeeze the juice from 1 half and chop the other half into small pieces.

2   Toss the potatoes, lemon juice, chopped lemon, garlic and oil together. Season, then arrange in a single layer in a shallow roasting tin and dot with the butter. Cook for 25–30 minutes, shaking the tin occasionally, until the potatoes are tender and golden brown. Stir in the olives just before serving.

Serves 4

Note: These tasty little potatoes are roasted with some of the best-loved flavours of the Mediterranean – garlic, lemon and olives. They go with almost anything.

Oven temperature 220°C

Barbecued Potato Skins

Preparation 10 mins **Cooking** 1 hr 10 mins **Calories** 270 **Fat** 12g

6 large potatoes, scrubbed
olive oil

1 Bake the potatoes in the oven for 1 hour or until tender. Remove from the oven and set aside until cool enough to handle. Cut the potatoes in half and scoop out the flesh, leaving a 5mm thick shell. Reserve the potato flesh for another use (see note). Cut the potato skins into large pieces and brush with oil.

2 Preheat the barbecue to a medium heat.

3 Cook the potato skins on a lightly oiled barbecue grill for 5–8 minutes each side or until crisp and golden. Serve with a dip of your choice.

Serves 6

Note: The reserved potato flesh can be used to make a potato salad to serve at your barbecue. It can also be used a potato curry, a topping on a cottage pie, or to make croquettes.

Glossary

Acidulated water: water with added acid, such as lemon juice or vinegar, which prevents discolouration of ingredients, particularly fruit or vegetables. The proportion of acid to water is 1 teaspoon per 300mL.

Al dente: Italian cooking term for ingredients that are cooked until tender but still firm to the bite; usually applied to pasta.

Américaine: method of serving seafood, usually lobster and monkfish, in a sauce flavoured with olive oil, aromatic herbs, tomatoes, white wine, fish stock, brandy and tarragon.

Anglaise: cooking style for simple cooked dishes such as boiled vegetables. Assiette anglaise is a plate of cold cooked meats.

Antipasto: Italian for 'before the meal', it denotes an assortment of cold meats, vegetables and cheeses, often marinated, served as an hors d'oeuvre. A typical antipasto might include salami, prosciutto, marinated artichoke hearts, anchovy fillets, olives, tuna fish and provolone cheese.

Au gratin: food sprinkled with breadcrumbs, often covered with cheese sauce and browned until a crisp coating forms.

Bain marie: a saucepan standing in a large pan which is filled with boiling water to keep liquids at simmering point. A double boiler will do the same job.

Balsamic vinegar: a mild, extremely fragrant, wine-based vinegar made in northern Italy. Traditionally, the vinegar is aged for at least seven years in a series of casks made of various woods.

Baste: to moisten food while it is cooking by spooning or brushing on liquid or fat.

Beat: to stir thoroughly and vigorously.

Beurre manie: equal quantities of butter and flour kneaded together and added, a little at a time, to thicken a stew or casserole.

bird: see *paupiette*.

Blanc: a cooking liquid made by adding flour and lemon juice to water in order to keep certain vegetables from discolouring as they cook.

Blanch: to plunge into boiling water and then, in some cases, into cold water. Fruits and nuts are blanched to remove skin easily.

Blanquette: a white stew of lamb, veal or chicken, bound with egg yolks and cream and accompanied by onion and mushrooms.

blend: to mix thoroughly.

Bonne femme: dishes cooked in the traditional French 'housewife' style. Chicken and pork *bonne femme* are garnished with bacon, potatoes and baby onion; fish *bonne femme* with mushrooms in a white-wine sauce.

Bouquet garni: a bunch of herbs, usually consisting of sprigs of parsley, thyme, marjoram, rosemary, a bay leaf, peppercorns and cloves, tied in muslin and used to flavour stews and casseroles.

Braise: to cook whole or large pieces of poultry, game, fish, meat or vegetables in a small amount of wine, stock or other liquid in a closed pot. Often the main ingredient is first browned in fat and then cooked in a low oven or very slowly on top of the stove. Braising suits tough meats and older birds and produces a mellow, rich sauce.

Broil: the American term for grilling food.

Brown: cook in a small amount of fat until brown.

Burghul (also bulgur): a type of cracked wheat, where the kernels are steamed and dried before being crushed.

Buttered: to spread with softened or melted butter.

Butterfly: to slit a piece of food in half horizontally, cutting it almost through so that when opened it resembles butterfly wings. Chops, large prawns and thick fish fillets are often butterflied so that they cook more quickly.

Buttermilk: a tangy, low-fat cultured milk product; its slight acidity makes it an ideal marinade base for poultry.

Calzone: a semicircular pocket of pizza dough, stuffed with meat or vegetables, sealed and baked.

Caramelise: to melt sugar until it is a golden-brown syrup.

Champignons: small mushrooms, usually canned.

Chasseur: French for 'hunter'; a French cooking style in which meat and chicken dishes are cooked with mushrooms, spring onions, white wine and often tomato.

Clarify: to melt butter and drain the oil off the sediment.

Coat: to cover with a thin layer of flour, sugar, nuts, crumbs, poppy or sesame seeds, cinnamon sugar or a few of the ground spices.

Concasser: to chop coarsely, usually tomatoes.

Confit: from the French verb *confire*, meaning to preserve, food that is made into a preserve by cooking very slowly and thoroughly until tender. In the case of meat, such as duck or goose, it is cooked in its own fat, and covered with the fat so that the meat does not come into contact with the air. Vegetables such as onions are good in confit.

Consommé: a clear soup usually made from beef.

Coulis: a thin purée, usually of fresh or cooked fruit or vegetables, which is soft enough to pour (in French *couler* means 'to run'). A coulis may be rough-textured or very smooth.

Court bouillon: the liquid in which fish, poultry or meat is cooked. It usually consists of water with bay leaf, onion, carrots and salt and freshly ground black pepper to taste. Other additives may include wine, vinegar, stock, garlic or spring (green) onions.

Couscous: cereal processed from semolina into pellets, traditionally steamed and served with meat and vegetables in the classic North African stew of the same name.

Cream: to make soft, smooth and creamy by rubbing with the back of a spoon or by beating with a mixer. Usually applied to fat and sugar.

Croutons: small toasted or fried cubes of bread.

Cruciferous vegetables: certain members of the mustard, cabbage and turnip families with cross-shaped flowers and strong aromas and flavours.

Crudités: raw vegetables, cut in slices or sticks to nibble plain or with a dipping sauce, or shredded vegetables tossed as salad with a simple dressing.

Cube: to cut into small pieces with six equal sides.

Curdle: to cause milk or sauce to separate into solid and liquid. Example, overcooked egg mixtures.

Daikon radish (also called mooli): a long white Japanese radish.

Dark sesame oil (also called Oriental sesame oil): dark polyunsaturated oil with a low burning point, used for seasoning. Do not replace with lighter sesame oil.

Deglaze: to dissolve congealed cooking juices or glaze on the bottom of a pan by adding a liquid, then scraping and stirring vigorously whilst bringing the liquid to the boil. Juices may be used to make gravy or to add to sauce.

Degrease: to skim grease from the surface of liquid. If possible the liquid should be chilled so the fat solidifies. If not, skim off most of the fat with a large metal spoon, then trail strips of paper towel on the surface of the liquid to remove any remaining globules.

Devilled: a dish or sauce that is highly seasoned with a hot ingredient such as mustard, Worcestershire sauce or cayenne pepper.

Dice: to cut into small cubes.

Dietary fibre: a plant-cell material that is undigested or only partially digested in the human body, but which promotes healthy digestion of other food matter.

Dissolve: mix a dry ingredient with liquid until absorbed.

Dredge: to coat with a dry ingredient, such as flour or sugar.

Drizzle: to pour in a fine thread-like stream over a surface.

Dust: to sprinkle or coat lightly with flour or icing sugar.

Dutch oven: a heavy casserole with a lid usually made from cast iron or pottery.

Emulsion: a mixture of two liquids that are not mutually soluble; for example, oil and water.

Entrée: in Europe, the 'entry' or hors d'oeuvre; in North America entree means the main course.

Fenugreek: a small, slender annual herb of the pea family. The seeds are spice. Ground fenugreek has a strong maple sweetness, spicy but bitter flavour and an aroma of burnt sugar.

Fillet: special cut of beef, lamb, pork or veal; breast of poultry and game; fish cut off the bone lengthwise.

Flake: to break into small pieces with a fork.

Flame: to ignite warmed alcohol over food.

Fold in: a gentle, careful combining of a light or delicate mixture with a heavier mixture, using a metal spoon.

Frenched: when fat and gristle is scraped and cut from meat on a bone, leaving the meaty part virtually fat free.

Fricassé: a dish in which poultry, fish or vegetables are bound together with a white or velouté sauce. In Britain and the United States, the name applies to an old-fashioned dish of chicken in a creamy sauce.

Galangal: A member of the ginger family, commonly known as Laos or Siamese ginger. It has a peppery taste with overtones of ginger.

Galette: sweet or savoury mixture shaped as a flat round.

Ganache: a filling or glaze made of full cream, chocolate, and/or other flavourings, often used to sandwich the layers of gourmet chocolate cakes

Garnish: to decorate food, usually with something edible.

Gastrique: caramelised sugar deglazed with vinegar and used in fruit-flavoured savoury sauces, in such dishes as duck with orange.

Ghee: butter, clarified by boiling. Commonly used in Indian cooking.

Glaze: a thin coating of beaten egg, syrup or aspic which is brushed over pastry, fruits or cooked meats.

Gluten: a protein in flour that is developed when dough is kneaded, making the dough elastic.

Gratin: a dish cooked in the oven or under the grill so that it develops a brown crust. Breadcrumbs or cheese may be sprinkled on top first. Shallow gratin dishes ensure a maximum area of crust.

Grease: to rub or brush lightly with oil or fat.

Infuse: to immerse herbs, spices or other flavourings in hot liquid to flavour it. Infusion takes 2–5 minutes depending on the flavouring. The liquid should be very hot but not boiling.

Jardinière: a garnish of garden vegetables, typically carrots, pickling onions, French beans and turnips.

Joint: to cut poultry, game or small animals into serving pieces by dividing at the joint.

Julienne: to cut food into match-like strips.

Lights: lungs of an animal, used in various meat preparations such as pates and faggots.

Line: to cover the inside of a container with paper, to protect or aid in removing mixture.

Knead: to work dough using heel of hand with a pressing motion, while stretching and folding the dough.

Macerate: to soak food in liquid to soften.

Marinade: a seasoned liquid, usually an oil and acid mixture, in which meats or other foods are soaked to soften and give more flavour.

Marinara: Italian 'sailor's style' cooking that does not apply to any particular combination of ingredients. Marinara tomato sauce for pasta is the most familiar.

Marinate: to let food stand in a marinade to season and tenderise.

Mask: to cover cooked food with sauce.

Melt: to heat until liquified.

Mince: to grind into very small pieces.

Mix: to combine ingredients by stirring.

Monounsaturated fats: one of three types of fats found in foods. It is believed these fats do not raise the level of cholesterol in the blood.

Naan: a slightly leavened bread used in Indian cooking.

Niçoise: a garnish of tomatoes, garlic and black olives; a salad with anchovy, tuna and French beans is typical.

Noisette: small 'nut' of lamb cut from boned loin or rack that is rolled, tied and cut in neat slices. Noisette also means flavoured with hazelnuts, or butter cooked to a nut brown colour.

Non-reactive pan: a cooking pan whose surface does not chemically react with food. Materials used include stainless steel, enamel, glass and some alloys.

Normande: a cooking style for fish, with a garnish of prawn, mussels and mushrooms in a white-wine cream sauce; for poultry and meat, a sauce with cream, calvados and apple.

Olive oil: various grades of oil extracted from olives. Extra virgin olive oil has a full, fruity flavour and the lowest acidity. Virgin olive oil is slightly higher in acidity and lighter in flavour. Pure olive oil is a processed blend of olive oils and has the highest acidity and lightest taste.

Panade: a mixture for binding stuffings and dumplings, notably quenelles (fish rissoles), often of choux pastry or simply breadcrumbs. A panade may also be made of frangipane, puréed potatoes or rice.

Papillote: to cook food in oiled or buttered greasepoof paper or aluminum foil. Also a decorative frill to cover bone ends of chops and poultry drumsticks.

Parboil: to boil or simmer until part cooked (i.e. cooked further than when blanching).

Pare: to cut away outside covering.

Pâté: a paste of meat or seafood used as a spread for toast or crackers.

Paupiette: a thin slice of meat, poultry or fish spread with a savoury stuffing and rolled. In the United States this is also called 'bird' and in Britain an 'olive'.

Peel: to strip away outside covering.

Plump: to soak in liquid or moisten thoroughly until full and round.

Poach: to simmer gently in enough hot liquid to cover, using care to retain shape of food.

Polyunsaturated fat: one of the three types of fats found in food. These exist in large quantities in such vegetable oils as safflower, sunflower, corn and soya bean. These fats lower the level of cholesterol in the blood.

Purée: a smooth paste, usually of vegetables or fruits, made by putting foods through a sieve, food mill or liquefying in a blender or food processor.

Ragout: traditionally a well-seasoned, rich stew containing meat, vegetables and wine. Nowadays, a term applied to any stewed mixture.

Ramekins: small oval or round individual baking dishes.

Reconstitute: to put moisture back into dehydrated foods by soaking in liquid.

Reduce: to cook over a very high heat, uncovered, until the liquid is reduced by evaporation.

Refresh: to cool hot food quickly, either under running water or by plunging it into iced water, to stop it cooking. Particularly for vegetables and occasionally for shellfish.

Rice vinegar: mild, fragrant vinegar that is less sweet than cider vinegar and not as harsh as distilled malt vinegar. Japanese rice vinegar is milder than the Chinese variety.

Roulade: a piece of meat, usually pork or veal, that is spread with stuffing, rolled and often braised or poached. A roulade may also be a sweet or savoury mixture that is baked in a Swiss-roll tin or paper case, filled with a contrasting filling, and rolled.

Roux: A binding for sauces, made with flour and butter or another fatty substance, to which a hot liquid is added. A roux-based sauce may be white, blond or brown, depending on how the butter has been cooked.

Rubbing-in: a method of incorporating fat into flour, by use of fingertips only. Also incorporates air into mixture.

Safflower oil: the vegetable oil that contains the highest proportion of polyunsaturated fats.

Salsa: a juice derived from the main ingredient being cooked, or a sauce added to a dish to enhance its flavour. In Italy the term is often used for pasta sauces; in Mexico the name usually applies to uncooked sauces served as an accompaniment, especially to corn chips.

Saturated fats: one of the three types of fats found in foods. These exist in large quantities in animal products, coconut and palm oils; they raise the level of cholesterol in the blood. As high cholesterol levels may cause heart disease, saturated-fat consumption is recommended to be less than 15 percent of calories provided by the daily diet.

Sauté: to cook or brown in small amount of hot fat.

Scald: to bring just to boiling point, usually for milk. Also to rinse with boiling water.

School prawns: delicious eaten just on their own. Smaller prawn than bay, tiger or king. They have a mild flavour, low oiliness and high moisture content, they make excellent cocktails.

Score: to mark food with cuts, notches or lines to prevent curling or to make food more attractive.

Sear: to brown surface quickly over high heat in hot dish.

Seasoned flour: flour with salt and pepper added.

Sift: to shake a dry, powdered substance through a sieve or sifter to remove any lumps and give lightness.

Simmer: to cook food gently in liquid that bubbles steadily just below boiling point so that the food cooks in even heat without breaking up.

Singe: to quickly flame poultry to remove all traces of feathers after plucking.

Skim: to remove a surface layer (often of impurities and scum) from a liquid with a metal spoon or small ladle.

Slivered: sliced in long, thin pieces, usually refers to nuts, especially almonds.

Souse: to cover food, particularly fish, in wine vinegar and spices and cook slowly; the food is cooled in the same liquid. Sousing gives food a pickled flavour.

Steep: to soak in warm or cold liquid in order to soften food and draw out strong flavours or impurities.

Stir-fry: to cook thin slices of meat and vegetable over a high heat in a small amount of oil, stirring constantly to even cooking in a short time. Traditionally cooked in a wok; however, a heavy-based frying pan may be used.

Stock: the liquid that results from cooking meat, bones and/or vegetables in water to make a base for soups and other recipes. You can substitute stock cubes for fresh bouillon, but those on a reduced sodium diet will need to take note of the salt content on the packet.

Stud: to adorn with; for example, baked ham studded with whole cloves.

Sugo: an Italian sauce made from the liquid or juice extracted from fruit or meat during cooking.

Sweat: to cook sliced or chopped food, usually vegetables, in a little fat and no liquid over very low heat. Foil is pressed on top so that the food steams in its own juices, usually before being added to other dishes.

Thicken: to make a liquid thicker by mixing together arrowroot, cornflour or flour with an equal amount of cold water and pouring it into hot liquid, cooking and stirring until thickened.

Timbale: a creamy mixture of vegetables or meat baked in a mould. French for 'kettledrum'; also denotes a drum-shaped baking dish.

Toss: to gently mix ingredients with two forks or fork and spoon.

Total fat: the individual daily intake of all three fats previously described in this glossary. Nutritionists recommend that fats provide no more than 35 percent of the energy in the diet.

Vine leaves: tender, lightly flavoured leaves of the grapevine, used in ethnic cuisine as wrappers for savoury mixtures. As the leaves are usually packed in brine, they should be well rinsed before use.

Whip: to beat rapidly, incorporate air and produce expansion.

Zest: thin outer layer of citrus fruits containing the aromatic citrus oil. It is usually thinly pared with a vegetable peeler, or grated with a zester or grater to separate it from the bitter white pith underneath.

Weights and Measures

Cooking is not an exact science; one does not require finely calibrated scales, pipettes and scientific equipment to cook, yet the conversion to metric measures in some countries and its interpretations must have intimidated many a good cook.

In the recipes weights are given for ingredients such, as meats, fish, poultry and some vegetables, but in normal cooking a few ounces or grams one way or another will not affect the success of your dish.

Although recipes have been tested using the Australian Standard 250mL cup, 20mL tablespoon and 5mL teaspoon, they will work just as well with the US and Canadian 8fl oz cup, or the UK 300mL cup. We have used graduated cup measures in preference to tablespoon measures so that proportions are always the same. Where tablespoon measures have been given, they are not crucial measures, so using the smaller tablespoon of the US or UK will not affect the recipe's success. At least we all agree on the teaspoon size.

For breads, cakes and pastries, the only area which might cause concern is where eggs are used, as proportions will then vary. If working with a 250mL or 300mL cup, use large eggs (65g/2$\frac{1}{4}$oz), adding a little more liquid to the recipe for 300mL cup measures if it seems necessary. Use the medium-sized eggs (55g/2oz) with 8fl oz cup measure. A graduated set of measuring cups and spoons is recommended, the cups in particular for measuring dry ingredients. Remember to level such ingredients to ensure an accurate quantity.

English Measures
All measurements are similar to Australian with two exceptions: the English cup measures 300mL/10$\frac{1}{2}$ fl oz, whereas the American and Australian cup measure 250mL/8$\frac{3}{4}$fl oz. The English tablespoon (the Australian dessertspoon) measures 14.8mL / $\frac{1}{2}$ fl oz against Australian tablespoon of 20mL/$\frac{3}{4}$fl oz. The Imperial measurement is 20fl oz to the pint, 40fl oz a quart and 160fl oz one gallon.

American Measures
The American reputed pint is 16fl oz, a quart is equal to 32fl oz and the American gallon, 128fl oz. The American tablespoon is equal to 14.8mL/$\frac{1}{2}$ fl oz, the teaspoon is 5mL/$\frac{1}{6}$ fl oz. The cup measure is 250 mL/8$\frac{3}{4}$ fl oz.

Dry Measures
All the measures are level, so when you have filled a cup or spoon, level it off with the edge of a knife. The scale below is the 'cook's equivalent'; it is not an exact conversion of metric to imperial measurement. To calculate the exact metric equivalent yourself, multiply onces x 28.349523 to obtain grams, or divide 28.349523 grams to obtain onces.

Metric grams (g), kilograms (kg)	Imperial ounces (oz), pound (lb)
15g	$\frac{1}{2}$oz
20g	$\frac{1}{3}$oz
30g	1oz
55g	2oz
85g	3oz
115g	4oz/$\frac{1}{4}$ lb
125g	4$\frac{1}{2}$oz
140/145g	5oz
170g	6oz
200g	7oz
225g	8oz/$\frac{1}{2}$ lb
315g	11oz
340g	12oz/$\frac{3}{4}$ lb
370g	13oz
400g	14oz
425g	15oz
455g	16oz/1 lb
1,000g/1kg	35.3oz/2.2 lb
1.5kg	3.33 lb

Oven Temperatures
The Celsius temperatures given here are not exact; they have been rounded off and are given as a guide only. Follow the manufacturer's temperature guide, relating it to oven description given in the recipe. Remember gas ovens are hottest at the top, electric ovens at the bottom and convection-fan forced ovens are usually even throughout. We included Regulo numbers for gas cookers which may assist. To convert °C to °F multiply °C by 9 and divide by 5 then add 32.

	C°	F°	Gas regulo
Very slow	120	250	1
Slow	150	300	2
Moderately slow	160	325	3
Moderate	180	350	4
Moderately hot	190–200	370–400	5–6
Hot	210–220	410–440	6–7
Very hot	230	450	8
Super hot	250–290	475–500	9–10

Cup Measurements

One cup is equal to the following weights.

	Metric	Imperial
Almonds, flaked	85g	3oz
Almonds, slivered, ground	125g	4$\frac{1}{2}$oz
Almonds, kernel	155g	5$\frac{1}{2}$oz
Apples, dried, chopped	125g	4$\frac{1}{2}$oz
Apricots, dried, chopped	190g	6$\frac{3}{4}$oz
Breadcrumbs, packet	125g	4$\frac{1}{2}$oz
Breadcrumbs, soft	55g	2oz
Cheese, grated	115g	4oz
Choc bits	155$\frac{1}{2}$g	5oz
Coconut, desiccated	90g	3oz
Cornflakes	30g	1oz
Currants	155$\frac{1}{2}$g	5oz
Flour	115g	4oz
Fruit, dried (mixed, sultanas etc)	170g	6 oz
Ginger, crystallised, glace	250g	8oz
Honey, treacle, golden syrup	315g	11oz
Mixed peel	225g	8oz
Nuts, chopped	115g	4oz
Prunes, chopped	225g	8oz
Rice, cooked	155g	5$\frac{1}{2}$oz
Rice, uncooked	225g	8oz
Rolled oats	90g	3oz
Sesame seeds	115g	4oz
Shortening (butter, margarine)	225g	8oz
Sugar, brown	155g	5$\frac{1}{2}$oz
Sugar, granulated or caster	225g	8oz
Sugar, sifted icing	155g	5$\frac{1}{2}$oz
Wheatgerm	60g	2oz

Length

Some of us still have trouble converting imperial length to metric. In this scale, measures have been rounded off to the easiest-to-use and most acceptable figures. To obtain the exact metric equivalent in converting inches to centimetres, multiply inches by 2.54 whereby 1 inch equals 25.4 millimetres and 1 millimetre equals 0.03937 inches.

Cake Dish Sizes

Metric	15cm	18cm	20cm	23cm
Imperial	6in	7in	8in	9in

Loaf Dish Sizes

Metric	23 x 12cm	25 x 8cm	28 x 18cm
Imperial	9 x 5in	10 x 3in	11 x 7in

Liquid Measures

Metric millilitres (mL)	Imperial fluid ounce (fl oz)	Cup and Spoon
5mL	$\frac{1}{6}$ fl oz	1 teaspoon
20mL	$\frac{2}{3}$ fl oz	1 tablespoon
30mL	1 fl oz	1 tbsp + 2 tsp
55mL	2 fl oz	
63mL	2$\frac{1}{4}$ fl oz	$\frac{1}{4}$ cup
85mL	3 fl oz	
115mL	4 fl oz	
125mL	4$\frac{1}{2}$ fl oz	$\frac{1}{2}$ cup
150mL	5$\frac{1}{4}$ fl oz	
188mL	6$\frac{2}{3}$ fl oz	$\frac{3}{4}$ cup
225mL	8 fl oz	
250mL	8$\frac{3}{4}$ fl oz	1 cup
300mL	10$\frac{1}{2}$ fl oz	
370mL	13 fl oz	
400mL	14 fl oz	
438mL	15$\frac{1}{2}$ fl oz	1$\frac{3}{4}$ cups
455mL	16 fl oz	
500mL	17$\frac{1}{2}$ fl oz	2 cups
570mL	0 fl oz	
1 litre	35.3 fl oz	4 cups

Length Measures

Metric millimetres (mm), centimetres (cm)	Imperial inches (in), feet (ft)
5mm, 0.5cm	$\frac{1}{4}$ in
10mm, 1.0cm	$\frac{1}{2}$ in
20mm, 2.0cm	$\frac{3}{4}$ in
2.5cm	1in
5 cm	2in
7$\frac{1}{2}$ cm	3in
10cm	4in
12$\frac{1}{2}$ cm	5in
15cm	6in
18cm	7in
20cm	8in
23cm	9in
25cm	10in
28cm	11in
30cm	12in, 1 foot

Index